A Principal's Guide
To Special Education

David Bateman and C. Fred Bateman

GOVERNORS STATE UNIVERSITY
UNIVERSITY PARK, IL

Council for
Exceptional
Children

The voice and vision of special education

Library of Congress Cataloging-in-Publication Data

Bateman, David (David F.)
  A principal's guide to special education / David Bateman & C. Fred Bateman
      p. cm.
  Includes bibliographical references (p.) and index.
    ISBN 0-86586-426-8
Handicapped children—Education—United States—Handbooks, manuals, etc. 2. manuals,
etc. 3. School principals—United States—Handbooks, manuals, etc. I. Bateman, C. Fred. II.
Title.

LC4019.B34 2001
371.9'0973—dc21

ISBN 0-86586-426-8 (Second edition, revised and expanded)

Copyright 2006 by Council for Exceptional Children, 1110 North Glebe Road, Suite 300,
Arlington, Virginia 22201-5704

Stock No. P5779

First edition 2001
Second edition 2006

Printed in the United States of America

10   9   8   7   6   5   4   3   2

Contents

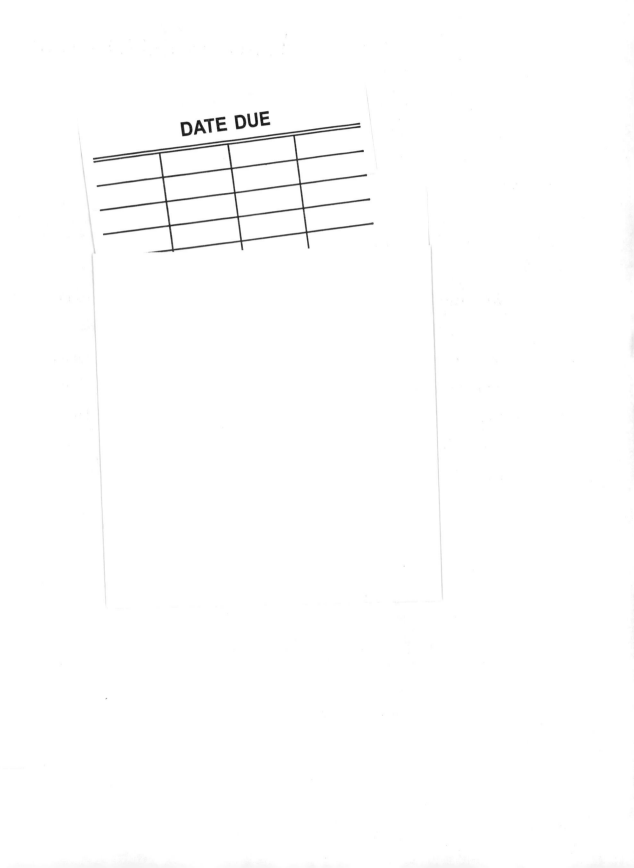

DATE DUE

Acknowledgments

We sincerely appreciate the efforts of two extraordinary principals in the preparation of this book. Dr. Jan Andrejco, Principal of Oscar Smith High School in Chesapeake, Virginia, and Dr. Alan Vaughan, former Principal of Greenbrier Intermediate School in Chesapeake, Virginia, provided the practitioner's view of special education. They both added considerable value to the final product, and their ideas and written contributions are embedded throughout the book.

About the Authors

David F. Bateman

Dr. Bateman has a B.A. in Government and Foreign Affairs from the University of Virginia, a M.Ed. in Special Education from the College of William and Mary, and a Ph.D. in Special Education from the University of Kansas. He has been a classroom teacher of students with learning disabilities, behavior disorders, mental retardation, and hearing impairments. He is a professor of special education at Shippensburg University of Pennsylvania, where he teaches courses in learning disabilities, special education law, and the introduction to special education. He is also a Due Process Hearing Officer for the Commonwealth of Pennsylvania and is Past-President of the Pennsylvania Federation Council for Exceptional Children. His latest area of research has been on the role of principals in special education.

C. Fred Bateman

Dr. Bateman has a B.A. and M.A. in Political Science from the University of Richmond, and an Ed.D. in Educational Administration from the University of Virginia. He has been a classroom teacher, supervisor, principal, and superintendent. Following his retirement after serving for 15 years as Superintendent of Schools for the City of Chesapeake, Virginia, he joined the faculty at Old Dominion University as the Distinguished Educator in Residence and Director of the Principals' Center of Hampton Roads. Currently, he is the Executive Director of the Urban Superintendents Association of America. He has written two other books and numerous articles on education. His latest area of research has been on the role of principals in special education.

Contributors

Susan Gilmartin Foltz is an assistant professor of special education at Shippensburg University. She has worked as a school psychologist for the past 25 years.

Kevin Koury is professor and chairperson of the Department of Special Education at California University of Pennsylvania.

Ron Miros works for the Pennsylvania Area Training and Technical Assistance Network emphasizing behaviors and mediation. He is a former director of special education.

Katherine Mitchem is an associate professor of special education and graduate program coordinator at California University of Pennsylvania.

Dorothy J. O'Shea is a professor of special education at Slippery Rock University.

Lawrence J. O'Shea is executive director of Intermediate Unit 1, Coal Center, Pennsylvania.

Johanna Rich Tesman is a school psychologist with the Capital Area Intermediate Unit in Summerdale, Pennsylvania.

1

Introduction:
What Do Principals
Need to Know About
Special Education?

A principal's responsibilities for servicing special education students include providing adequate facilities, selecting appropriately qualified staff, partnering with parents, and diligently scheduling students. The addition of high stakes testing and the mandates of the Individuals with Disabilities Education Improvement Act of 2004 (IDEA) and the No Child Left Behind Act of 2001 (NCLB) require careful analysis and monitoring to assure adequate yearly progress (AYP). State and federal mandates are successfully making us do what should have been done all along: ensuring that every student learns. Enhancing the communication and instructional skills of both general education and special education teachers through professional development and collaborative planning will create more successful opportunities for all students.

SEEKING SUPPORT AND ADVICE

It is wise to seek advice when unsure how to handle placement, IEP decisions, and testing of special needs students. Districts have special education administrators, specialists, and attorneys; the state department of education provides guidelines and advice; and the school board attorney may have a more local perspective. One commercial entity providing some clarity and guidance is LRP Resources, which can be reached at 1-800-341-7874. For more information see http://www.cec.sped.org/bk/catalog2/index.html. For additional resources from the Council for Exceptional Children see http://www.sped.org.

THE LOGISTICS OF SERVICING SPECIAL EDUCATION STUDENTS

Your *facility* needs to be equally accessible to all students, and, if necessary, you must seek modifications necessary to ensure equal access. Ensure that the location of classrooms and various activities (on different floors, outside, etc.) is planned in consideration of the needs of your students who require classroom accommodations or have mobility difficulties. Classroom space requirements vary depending on the type of class or program operating in the classroom. One size classroom does not fit all programs. Some special education classes require more square footage than the typical classroom, while others function well in a smaller space. When building a new school, considering the space needs for each program could result in financial savings. A class for students with more severe disabilities, requiring special equipment and the assignment of more adult staff and volunteers, needs more physical space to accommodate gross motor needs.

Similarly, *emergency and security plans* need to incorporate the particular needs of special education students, some of whom will require special provisions. A fire drill or more serious emergency can occur at any time during a school day. Preparing in advance for such a circumstance is essential to the safety of all students and staff members. After drafting your emergency plan, or reviewing it annually, remember to identify those students requiring additional assistance. You must be able to identify these students' location within the building at any time of day. Although self-contained special education classes are staffed at a higher ratio, there are not always enough staff members assigned to evacuate or otherwise assist all of the students quickly and safely.

Constructing a school master schedule is a complex process. The size of the special education department has a direct effect on the master schedule for several reasons. Students with disabilities typically require more flexibility, as their schedules may need to include adaptive classes or remedial courses in addition to inclusion classes. Particularly in the secondary school environment, it is important to schedule classes for special education students first when you create the master schedule, not last.

HOW CAN THIS BOOK HELP PRINCIPALS?

➠ **Chapter 2** describes some of the issues surrounding developing an effective teaching staff. As more students are identified as having special needs, and with expectations that they will be included in the general education classroom, the role of the special education teacher takes on a new responsibility. Special education teachers can assist general education teachers in identifying simple classroom modifications and accommodations that help struggling students succeed, such as preferential seating, allowing additional time to complete work, reading test questions aloud, providing step-by-step instructions, and presenting information in ways that adapt to different learning styles.

➠ **Chapter 3** provides a valuable introduction to special education law, offering a historical perspective on current trends in educating students of varying abilities and disabilities. It also covers Section 504 of the Rehabilitation

Act, the Americans with Disabilities Act, and the Family Education Rights and Privacy Act (FERPA).

➠ **Chapter 4** discusses the No Child Left Behind Act of 2001 (NCLB). Few things have impacted education as dramatically as the accountability movement. Beginning with *A Nation At Risk* (1983) and continuing through NCLB, the call for higher standards has resounded throughout education. This call has been keenly felt in the special education classroom.

Principals face a myriad of conflicting guidelines: NCLB seems to conflict with IDEA; providing an individualized education program (IEP) that meets each child's individual needs seems to conflict with the requirement to make adequate yearly progress (AYP). The expectation of NCLB is that all students will achieve at grade level, including the vast majority of special education students. There are no clear and easy answers here. There have been and will continue to be court challenges to NCLB.

The history of the accountability movement at both the state and federal levels has generally been one of raising the bar to a much higher level than before in the face of political pressure, and then some adjustment to a level that is more attainable, or, at a minimum, allowing a longer time period to meet the higher level. While this adjustment period plays out, the principal can be placed in a very difficult position in trying to interpret IDEA and NCLB when the two seem to be in conflict with each other. There are times when any principal's ethics can be sorely tested. Placement of a particular special education student and how standardized testing is handled can be factors that impact accreditation based on state standards, as well as the difference between making AYP and not making AYP.

➠ **Chapter 5** discusses identifying and assessing students for special education services. It provides advice on what should be done before referrals, meeting with parents, and after the meeting to ensure students with disabilities receive the education they need based on their evaluation.

➠ **Chapter 6** examines of the process of developing an IEP. As a principal, you must be able to oversee the effective development and implementation of IEPs. Many general education teachers may be unfamiliar with all the requirements of supporting a student's IEP, but IDEA 2004 mandates representation of general education teachers on IEP teams. Many IEP accommodations enable the child to demonstrate mastery of the material, just not always in the same way as his classmates.

➠ **Chapter 7** discusses the inclusion of special education students in the general education classroom. What guidelines does the law provide? The *continuum of alternative placements* is important to keep in mind when talking about inclusion. It is also an important part of the Council for Exceptional Children's (CEC) policy on inclusive schools.

> CEC believes a continuum of services must be available for all children, youth, and young adults. CEC also believes that the concept of inclusion is a meaningful goal to be pursued in our schools and communities. In addition, CEC believes children, youth, and young adults with disabilities should be served

whenever possible in general education classrooms in inclusive neighborhood schools and community settings.

➠ **Chapter 8** Chapter 8 discusses development and administration of school discipline plans that accommodate students with disabilities. It also highlights the recent changes to the requirements for disciplining students with disabilities as a result of IDEA 2004.

➠ **Chapter 9** describes due process; the required procedures and notifications that govern the rights of both parents and school in the delivery of special education services. This chapter also discusses the procedures for preparation for a due process hearing if an amicable solution cannot be reached between the school district and the parents.

As a principal, you may find the various issues pertaining to special education teachers, parents, and students challenging. Even the interaction of special education programs with general education teachers, parents, and students can sometimes become an issue.

In providing special education services, the principal should always do what is best for the child. This may sound very simplistic, but this simple goal can get lost from sight when viewpoints sharply differ and emotions run high. In the event that a special education situation should require due process or even go to court, there is no more defensible position than that of doing what was best for the child. With this goal in mind, as a principal you continue to have a positive impact on the lives of your students.

2

What Does a Principal Need to Know About Staffing?

RON MIROS

Selecting staff to teach students with disabilities is not a consideration limited to hiring special education teachers and special education teacher assistants. The needs of students with disabilities need to be considered when hiring all general education teachers, assistant principals, teacher assistants, resource personnel, and support staff, because your students will interact with all of these staff members. Your staff should have high expectations for all students, have some knowledge of the Individuals with Disabilities Education Act (IDEA) and special education law, accept students with all types of disabilities, and be familiar with current instructional strategies. A carefully planned staff development program is helpful in filling the voids.

Your support staff might include physical therapists, counselors, occupational therapists, teacher assistants, nurses, vision specialists, mobility specialists, speech therapists, and non-English-language or sign language interpreters; best practices for hiring teaching staff apply to these members of your team as well.

SPECIAL EDUCATION TEACHERS

Special education teachers face unique challenges in the education environment. The gains their students make are often very small and come only after intense efforts. They have to individualize instruction to find success, because they usually work with students who have widely varying needs. They need to listen to the concerns of parents who may be demanding, disinterested, or ungrateful (although most are conscientious and very thankful for the caring of the special education teacher). Some special educators feel isolated within the school, since their students are often a small percentage of the total school population and frequently left out of many aspects of the mainstream life of the school. Special education teachers meet these challenges on a daily basis because they care deeply, often passionately, about their students.

Integrating the Special Education Teacher

As a principal, you need to set the example to the rest of the staff that special education is an integral part of the educational program at your school. The key is establishing a philosophy that integrates the special education component into decisions from the beginning, not as an afterthought. Not only do special education teachers sometimes feel disconnected from the rest of the staff, but general education teachers often feel disconnected from special education teachers as well. The main idea to get across is that the teachers have more in common than they do differences. Special education teachers are teaching the same material and can benefit from the same inservice activities. Special education teachers can provide invaluable inservice and resources to staff members seeking strategies to use with struggling students, some of whom may be students with undiagnosed learning disabilities. IDEA 2004's support for inclusive classrooms requires general education teachers to be able to adapt to differing learning styles and develop classroom accommodations and modifications—often before a student is even evaluated for special education services.

Working with general education teachers before the first day of classes, the special education teacher can help them prepare for special education students in the class. For a long time, special education teachers wanted anonymity for the special education students, to give them a "fair" chance. For many reasons, anonymity is not the best plan; with IDEA requirements that general education teachers participate in individualized education program (IEP) meetings and development, it is also against the law. General education teachers need as much information as is available to provide the best education for all students. At a minimum, they need to be familiar with the accommodations required by a student's IEP, and any medical information or behavioral information pertaining to the classroom and learning—all of which are considered essential to the student's success in the classroom. If a student fails to progress, it is the responsibility of the special education teacher to schedule an IEP team meeting and discuss appropriate interventions for the student.

Special education teachers should communicate regularly with general education teachers about specific students, and take the time to listen to and discuss concerns.

There are a variety of ways to improve the integration of the special education staff into your school's activities, and enhance cooperation between staff members:

✓ Assign special education teachers as coaches and sponsors, to serve on committees, attend extracurricular activities, and participate in professional development programs.

✓ One school's special education department volunteered to teach a portion of the school's gifted and talented education program, sponsored an annual "Super Science Friday" program (in which community members demonstrate how they use science in their professions), and became involved with many other activities that have made them an integral part of the fabric of the school.

✓ Ensure that general education teachers learn about the special education teachers' jobs, the special education program, and the types of student needs the program is addressing.

✓ Provide professional development activities for general education teachers on special education topics. The topics could include special education law, how to provide accommodations, how to participate in an IEP conference, the special education process.

It is the responsibility of the principal to provide the structure and opportunities in which special education teachers can become a part of the total school experience, and develop an environment of acceptance and cooperation. Providing both direction and time will help the staff reach these goals.

MANAGING LARGER SPECIAL EDUCATION POPULATIONS BY CO-TEACHING

Inclusion, as discussed in Chapter 7, refers to the placement of special education students in a general education classroom. When a school's special education population is 10% or less of the total student population, the typical inclusion and resource models seem to work well. In these typical models, a student is scheduled for at least one resource class with the special education teacher and all other classes in the general education classroom. However, when the special education population exceeds 10% and approaches 15% or more, the general education classes begin to reach critical mass with special education students. Expecting a general education teacher to effectively manage a classroom of 30 students consisting of 10 to 12 special education students is impractical. Implementing a co-teaching model can be beneficial to both students and staff.

A co-teaching model utilizes the expertise of the general education teacher and special education teacher in the same classroom, working together to teach all students. The most effective co-teaching model has provisions for both of the teachers to teach the class. The least effective co-teaching model utilizes the special education teacher as a teacher assistant in the general education classroom, assisting rather than teaching.

Once students see both teachers teaching, the teachers gain credibility and students are more open to learning and accepting help. The biggest hurdle to overcome is for the general education teacher to give up class time to the special education teacher. The special education teacher can carry out some or all of the following suggested teaching responsibilities:

✓ Conduct the warm-up activity.

✓ Direct the independent practice activity.

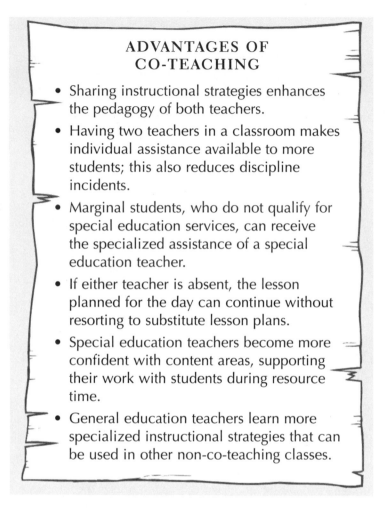

ADVANTAGES OF CO-TEACHING

- Sharing instructional strategies enhances the pedagogy of both teachers.
- Having two teachers in a classroom makes individual assistance available to more students; this also reduces discipline incidents.
- Marginal students, who do not qualify for special education services, can receive the specialized assistance of a special education teacher.
- If either teacher is absent, the lesson planned for the day can continue without resorting to substitute lesson plans.
- Special education teachers become more confident with content areas, supporting their work with students during resource time.
- General education teachers learn more specialized instructional strategies that can be used in other non-co-teaching classes.

✓   Conduct the review or summary at the end of the lesson.

✓   Assign homework.

✓   Conduct the homework review.

In this model, the general education teacher continues to provide the direct instruction and the special education teacher contributes to classroom instruction. Collaborative planning by the two teachers is essential for seamless lesson delivery.

If this co-teaching model were adopted, the special education teacher's schedule might consist of one co-teaching block and the remaining blocks resource time, during which the special education teacher provides support to special education students.

One caution for the co-teaching model in a school with a large special education population is that resource class size will increase slightly. The benefits of students attending general education classes and receiving more individual assistance in those classes far outweigh the drawback of larger resource classes.

Developing a Co-Teaching Program

To launch a successful co-teaching program, select two teachers who are open to trying a new idea and are less likely to be territorial in sharing a classroom. Planning together and sharing a classroom and instructional responsibilities requires the cooperation and flexibility of both teachers. Once it works well, other teachers realize the benefits and become anxious to begin co-teaching.

In order for a general education teacher and a special education teacher to teach together as a team, they must have time to plan together. Because you don't want to overload one class with students who have disabilities, the special education teacher is usually paired with two teachers at different times during the school day. (The teacher may be co-teaching in one class in the morning while a special education teacher assistant is working with the other inclusion class, and then reverse their roles in the afternoon.) The special education teacher may therefore need to plan together with two or more other staff members. Scheduling a common planning time for these teachers is essential to the success of your program.

HIGHLY QUALIFIED TEACHERS (HQT)

The No Child Left Behind Act of 2001 (NCLB) requires special education teachers to be *highly qualified*. For more information, see Chapter 4 on No Child Left Behind. While the details may not be totally clear, this should be a concern for all secondary principals and personnel administrators. The legislation requires that special education teachers be highly qualified in and primary teachers of a core subject (English, math, science, or social studies). While some teachers may be highly qualified in two, three, or all four core subjects, others may be highly qualified in one core subject. A teacher's status as highly qualified can change from year to year, or even within a school year, based on student enrollment, transfer of one student, or an IEP change.

For example, Teacher A is assigned to 22 students throughout a day, providing primary instruction in English and science to 15 students and English only to 7 students in a pullout resource environment. Teacher A, therefore, is required to be highly qualified in English and science. During the school year, a new student transfers into Teacher A's class. The student's IEP requires that the student receive primary instruction in math in the resource room environment; Teacher A is now required to be highly qualified in English, science, *and math*.

As a principal, you have a dual concern: You need to both service students and meet the HQT requirements without overburdening any one teacher. By ensuring that your teachers are highly qualified in more than one subject, your students will receive more focused and specialized instruction (Figure 2-1), and you will have more flexibility in scheduling.

Students who do not receive instruction from a general education teacher in a core subject and whose IEP states that instruction in that core area is required must be taught by a highly qualified special education teacher in that subject. If a student in Teacher D's class receives instruction in English from a general education teacher and the IEP states that instruction in all core subjects should be provided, then Teacher D must be highly qualified in math, science, and social studies.

FIGURE 2-1. HIGHLY QUALIFIED RESOURCE TEACHERS

TEACHERS	ENGLISH	MATH	SCIENCE	SOCIAL STUDIES
A	✗		✗	
B	✗			✗
C		✗	✗	
D		✗		✗
E	✗	✗		
F	✗	✗		
G		✗	✗	
H	✗	✗		
I	✗			✗
J		✗	✗	

BEST PRACTICES: HIRING, MENTORING, AND PROFESSIONAL DEVELOPMENT

Hiring Instructional Staff

The bottom line in hiring anyone is that you want to hire the most knowledgeable, competent, and cooperative person you can find. The more knowledgeable, competent, and cooperative your staff, the better your program is going to be. Your main goal in replacing staff or filling a brand new position is to find the most qualified candidate who meets the criteria of "knowledgeable, competent, and cooperative" and to do this in the most efficient and effective manner.

When interviewing potential candidates, your committee should not be too large or too small; generally, between three and six people, and representative of your special education staff, your general education staff, and your administration. You need staff representatives from special education, general education teacher, the school administration, and the special education. You want to get to know the candidate and also see how he or she will fit into the structure of your school.

Interview questions can cover such areas as lesson planning, familiarity with your state's curriculum, assessment and teaching strategies, instructional techniques, classroom management and discipline, and IEPs. Some schools invite candidates to prepare a demonstration lesson to illustrate practical applications of theory and approaches.

Mentoring New Employees

Most school districts today have some kind of mentoring program in place. Is yours designed to accommodate special education teachers? Mentoring the special education teacher is much different than mentoring a general education teacher. For one thing, your pool of veteran teachers from which to choose a mentor is much smaller.

Secondly, the kinds of paperwork and activities the special education teacher is expected to handle is very different from the general education elementary or secondary teacher's paperwork and activities. Matching the new teacher with a knowledgeable, competent, and friendly veteran is an essential ingredient to a new teacher's success.

It is also important to have control or influence over the handouts new employees receives. In most cases, there is a general packet of materials given to all staff whether they are general or special education, elementary or secondary. There is usually a dearth of specific information for the special education teacher. There are some good reasons for this.

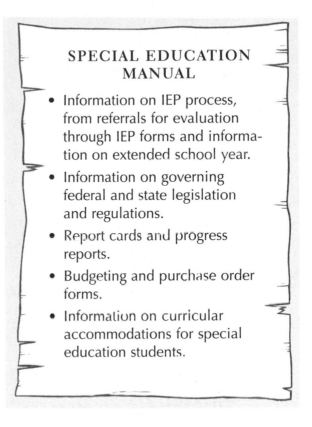

SPECIAL EDUCATION MANUAL

- Information on IEP process, from referrals for evaluation through IEP forms and information on extended school year.
- Information on governing federal and state legislation and regulations.
- Report cards and progress reports.
- Budgeting and purchase order forms.
- Information on curricular accommodations for special education students.

Special education law, regulations, and case law change frequently. By the time practice and procedure catch up, it is time to change again. Keeping up with these changes is challenging, even when you are a specialist. Additionally, most employees who have the responsibility of creating mentoring systems and orientation programs are not familiar with special education.

As principal, you need to remedy this situation for your new special education staff. Perhaps you can work with your district's supervisor of special education to compile together a special education manual, or elicit the support of a county consultant or state educational agency personnel. Your region or state may already have developed this sort of information for new teachers. One of your special education teachers might be willing to develop information that is more specific to your school. However you create or obtain one, a special education staff manual is an absolute necessity if you wish to run an efficient and effective special education program.

Professional Development

Your professional development program should focus on the teaching preparation and instructional procedures that you favor. You want to ensure that both new teachers and veterans are aware of current practices and approaches to

✓ Behavior management.

✓ Transitioning between discrete activities.

✓ Effective use of media and technology.

✓ Classroom accommodations and modifications.

✓ Student grouping, peer tutoring, and peer mentors.

✓ Maximizing instructional time.

✓ Lesson sequencing.

✓ Adapting materials.

You can explore options for inservice training, conferences, and meetings that provide the training your staff needs (see discussion of these training opportunities in the Chapter 7).

The staffing of a school with effective teachers is one of the most important tasks a principal will have. As any principal knows, finding (and keeping) quality teachers can be a daunting task. The information in this chapter can help you meet the needs of students with disabilities through the use of highly qualified teachers. The principal also has to be knowledgeable of the roles and responsibilities of the support staff who will be providing educational services. The principal must have high expectations for their job performance.

3

What Is
Special Education Law?

There are several important laws guiding the education of students with
disabilities. Understanding each will assist in providing appropriate services
in your school.

THE EDUCATION OF ALL HANDICAPPED
CHILDREN ACT OF 1975

This federal law, the precursor of the Individuals with Disabilities Education Act
(IDEA), required states to develop and implement policies to assure a free appro
priate public education to all children with disabilities. The law directed states to
establish procedures for identification, evaluation, and placement; introduced the
concept of educating students in the least restrictive environment; provided criteria for
developing, implementing and monitoring IEPs; and required shared decision making
and procedural safeguards. It also required states to provide related services and to
develop transition plans for students leaving school. The title of the Act is very specific, emphasizing the importance of including all children. Historically, schools had
excluded children with disabilities because they were perceived as not being able to
benefit from education or as not being "ready" for school. With this Act, Congress
stressed that no child was to be excluded from public education with his or her peers.

INDIVIDUALS WITH DISABILITIES EDUCATION ACT
OF 1990 (IDEA)

In 1990, Congress codified the Education of All Handicapped Children Act as the
Individuals with Disabilities Education Act (IDEA). Congress has the responsibility of
revisiting the law every 5 years to see how it is working, and to make changes when necessary. That is why, if you have been a principal for over 5 years, it seems the law is continually changing. The first significant point of the 1990 amendments is the rewording
of the Act's title. In 1975, the law used the term "handicapped children." The new ter-

ASSESSING CHILDREN WITH DISABILITIES

- All children must be tested in their primary language.
- IQ tests alone cannot be used for the placement of children into special education programs.
- Unvalidated tests cannot be used.
- Parents must be notified before any testing may begin (there are procedures for bypass if parents do not consent to testing).
- Group tests are not to be used for determining eligibility.
- Adaptive behavior must be taken into account when considering eligibility.

minology, "individuals with disabilities," reflects the philosophy that the individual should be recognized first and the condition second. Additionally, the new title emphasized the preference for the term "disability" over the label "handicap," which many people regarded as demeaning. This is the original law that has been amended and modified to the present day Individuals With Disabilities Education Act of 2004.

Definition of Disabilities

IDEA defines children with disabilities as those who have mental retardation, are hard of hearing, deaf, speech or language impaired, visually disabled, seriously emotionally disturbed, orthopedically impaired or other health impaired, autistic, deaf-blind, multihandicapped, or have specific learning disabilities or traumatic brain injury. IDEA definitions are not as broad or as inclusive as the definitions in Section 504 of the Rehabilitation Act of 1973. For example, an individual who is alcohol dependent could have a disability under Section 504 (they either have an impairment, have a record of an impairment, or are regarded as having an impairment), but would not be considered to have a disability under IDEA. IDEA definitions are categorical in nature, whereas definitions under Section 504 are functional in nature, meeting one of the three life-defining criteria.

Identification, Evaluation, and Placement

Historically, there have been problems in the testing and placement of children with disabilities, including things such as not testing in their primary language, not measuring adaptive behavior, or relying on a single test for classification and placement. These practices resulted in several court cases stipulating correct procedures for the assessment and classification of children with disabilities. Current law and legal decisions stipulate that school districts must seek out and evaluate each child with a suspected disability in their jurisdiction, and must implement procedures to screen preschool-age children for disabilities.

Procedures for notifying parents about testing can include announcements in the newspaper, as well as notices in grocery stores, gas stations, physicians' offices, and churches. These notices would have dates and locations for screening to determine eligibility for services before entering school at age five or six. Regardless of the age of the child, school districts must identify the specific nature of a child's disability and determine the type and extent of special education and related services required.

Additionally, the evaluation of the child must be an *individualized assessment* of all areas related to the suspected disability. For example, if a child has a suspected reading disability, the focus relates to the problems in reading; if the suspected problem is a math disability, the focus is on math. A team must make the eligibility decision, with at least one member of the team experienced in the suspected disability category. The job of the team is to determine whether a child is eligible for special education and related services. Districts must also notify parents of their right to an independent evaluation at public expense if they disagree with the results or procedures of the school district's evaluation. If the team finds the student eligi-

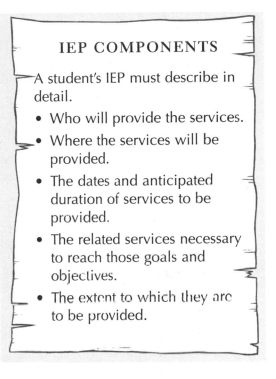

IEP COMPONENTS

A student's IEP must describe in detail.
- Who will provide the services.
- Where the services will be provided.
- The dates and anticipated duration of services to be provided.
- The related services necessary to reach those goals and objectives.
- The extent to which they are to be provided.

ble, an IEP needs to be developed based on the results of the assessments.

The eligibility process is repeated every 3 years. Historically, children were placed inappropriately in special education and remained there for the duration of their schooling. Therefore, the law mandates at least a 3-year or triennial evaluation, to determine that a child still qualifies for special education services.

After the individualized evaluation with a finding of eligibility, the team develops an IEP, a legal document describing the special education and related services designed to meet the needs of a child who has a disability. The IEP describes the child's present level of educational performance, and delineates goals and objectives based on this functioning. The IEP also defines objective criteria and evaluation procedures, and schedules for determining, on a regular basis (at least as regularly as nondisabled students get feedback), progress toward IEP goals.

The IEP team decides on and describes in the IEP the special education placement to be provided (this should not be decided until the IEP meeting), and the amount and location of participation with students who do not have disabilities. If a student is not going to participate with students without disabilities, the team must document why this will not occur, and when such placement might occur.

The IEP is more than a document outlining goals and objectives. It serves as a written commitment by the local education agency to provide the services.

Appropriate Education

Historically, students with disabilities were placed in a disability-specific classroom, whether that placement would provide them an "appropriate" education or not. The

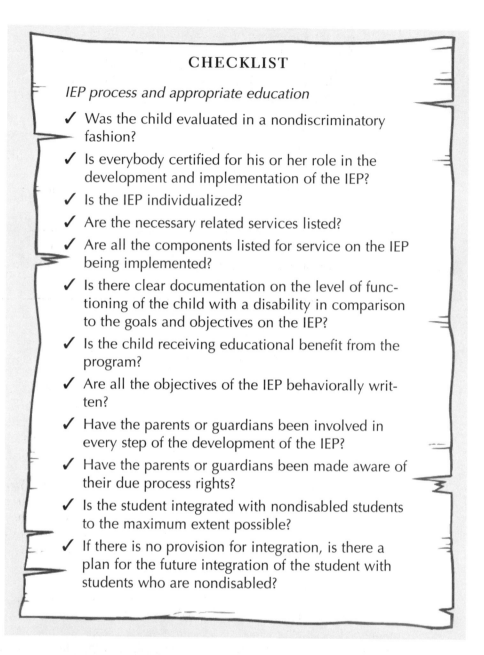

CHECKLIST

IEP process and appropriate education

✓ Was the child evaluated in a nondiscriminatory fashion?

✓ Is everybody certified for his or her role in the development and implementation of the IEP?

✓ Is the IEP individualized?

✓ Are the necessary related services listed?

✓ Are all the components listed for service on the IEP being implemented?

✓ Is there clear documentation on the level of functioning of the child with a disability in comparison to the goals and objectives on the IEP?

✓ Is the child receiving educational benefit from the program?

✓ Are all the objectives of the IEP behaviorally written?

✓ Have the parents or guardians been involved in every step of the development of the IEP?

✓ Have the parents or guardians been made aware of their due process rights?

✓ Is the student integrated with nondisabled students to the maximum extent possible?

✓ If there is no provision for integration, is there a plan for the future integration of the student with students who are nondisabled?

term *appropriate*, however, has caused a great deal of confusion both before and after the implementation of the original Education for All Handicapped Children Act. What one parent, supervisor, principal, or teacher finds appropriate, another might deem completely inappropriate.

State and local education agencies need to show that they are providing an appropriate education for all students with disabilities in their jurisdiction to receive federal funding for special education. *Appropriate education* is a process definition; if the district follows a certain process in the development and implementation of the IEP, then the student should be receiving an acceptable result. This is why it is imperative that principals have a full and complete understanding of the IEP process.

Additionally, a principal needs to become an active participant to ensure not only that the district follows appropriate procedures, but also that the student receives an appropriate education. The burden is on the professionals who develop and implement the IEP to show that it was based on correct information. Districts also need to show it was properly developed and implemented, and that proper monitoring occurred during its implementation.

Least Restrictive Environment

For many years, the term *mainstreaming* was used to describe circumstances in which special education teachers integrated students with disabilities into general education classrooms or activities.

The term "mainstreaming" does not exist in any legislation; it is a term popularized in special education literature and relates to placement of students with disabilities.

IDEA 2004 states:

> It is the purpose of this Act to assure that all handicapped children have available to them . . . a free appropriate public education which emphasizes special education and related services designed to meet their unique needs. To the maximum extent appropriate, handicapped children, including children in public or private institutions or other care facilities, are educated with children who are not handicapped. (20 U.S.C. § 1401 (b) (1)-(5))

The current term used to describe this principle is *inclusion*. There are several differences between mainstreaming and inclusion. One notable difference is that in mainstreaming, students with disabilities are integrated into the general education classroom after they have improved their performance in the special education classroom. In inclusion, the presumption is that the student will be in the general education classroom with supports, unless it is shown that the child cannot benefit from education in the general classroom.

It is not the intent of this chapter to discuss full inclusion (see Chapter 7), rather to clarify the law. The law states that "schools must maintain a continuum of alternative placements such as special classes, resource rooms, and itinerant instruction to meet the needs of the disabled" (34 C.F.R. § 300.115). The services and the location of those services are listed on the IEP. Appropriate placement for some students may be in the general education classroom with little additional assistance from special education teachers, while other students require residential settings, totally separated from nondisabled students.

Often forgotten is that the law stipulates that services are to follow students; that is, services must be tailored to the unique needs of the individual, and provided in the most appropriate setting. It is not acceptable for students to be assigned solely those services that are designated for a particular disability or those programs that are available or convenient. Just because a student is identified as having severe mental retardation does not mean the student has to be placed in a self-contained classroom when a partial-day program or a resource room might be better suited to that child. Every school district needs to offer a continuum of services, including everything from the general education classroom to hospital-type settings.

Related Services

In addition to specific educational services for students with disabilities, children may require other *related services* in order to benefit from special education, including:

> Transportation, and such . . . other supportive services (including speech pathology and audiology), psychological services, physical and occupational therapy, recreation, including therapeutic recreation and social work services, and medical and counseling services, including rehabilitation counseling, (except that such medical services shall be for diagnostic and evaluation purposes only) as may be required to assist a child with a disability to benefit from special education, and includes the early identification and assessment of disabling conditions in children. (34 C.F.R. § 300.34)

Several conditions must be met before a child receives related services. First, a child must be eligible for special education services. In the absence of eligibility, the student cannot receive related services—even if the student who might benefit from related services. Second, only those services necessary to help the student with a disability benefit from special education must be provided, regardless of how easily a school nurse or lay person can furnish them. For example, if a particular medication or treatment may appropriately be administered to a child other than during the school day, the school is not required to provide nursing services to administer it. Third, the regulations state that medical services must be provided only if they can be performed by a nurse or other qualified person, not if a physician is required.

Just as classroom placement is individually determined for the child with a disability, the need for related services should be determined in the same manner and listed on the IEP. IDEA requires school districts to delineate in a student's IEP the related services needed, regardless of whether they are currently available.

Parental Involvement

For many years, parents were shut out of the decision-making process because it was assumed that they were the cause of the child's disability (e.g., Bruno Bettleheim and autism). Professionals viewed parents as ignorant of their children's educational needs, and felt that educators knew what was best for the children. Parents and guardians have essential information about their children with disabilities. Legislators realized this and outlined provisions in IDEA 2004 ensuring parental participation in the special education process. They enumerated procedures for notification, access to records (as in FERPA), consultation, and participation in advisory panels.

Shared decision making protects the rights of students by ensuring there is someone involved in the process who has a long-term interest in the child. It could be argued that what affects the student with a disability also affects the parent; most educators now regard parents as important stakeholders.

IDEA states parents need to be aware of and consent to every step of the process. This includes the initial evaluation, the eligibility meeting, development of the IEP, annual reviews, and the triennial evaluation process. Parents also need access to all the records kept on their children and assurances about confidentiality.

The early childhood amendments to IDEA have added requirements for parent involvement: Districts must establish a public awareness campaign, a comprehensive child find program, and a central director of information. School systems also have an obligation to work with a family when a child is identified as needing special education services. Early childhood personnel should start working with families as early as possible, providing the child with as much assistance as possible before he or she enters school for the first time.

Children with disabilities who are participating in early childhood special education receive an individualized family services plan (IFSP). Similar to the development of the IEP, the IFSP includes a heavy family component because of the realization that families play a vital role in the development and nurturing of children. One component is working with the family to help them meet their child's needs. This can be accomplished either through training family members to carry out specific duties or by collaborating with them to determine the best methods for working with their child who has a disability. The IFSP is more than just an IEP with a family twist, though; it is a multidisciplinary document designed to enhance children's development and minimize delays by enhancing the family's capacity to meet the child's needs.

Another important component of the early childhood amendments is the realization that one service provider does not have to be the sole organization working to address circumstances for the child with a disability and the family members. Ideally, multiple agencies must work together to provide combinations of approaches and interventions.

Due Process

One main component of special education law is the opportunity for parental decision making on all the different levels affecting a child's eligibility for special education services. If a parent or guardian disapproves of the methods used for determining eligibility, or the educational programming for a child with disabilities, or disapproves of the resulting decisions, due process procedures allow interested parties to challenge the school system.

Appropriate notification is one essential element of procedural due process. The law is very specific about requirements relating to notice. The law requires written notice before the schools can propose to initiate or change, or refuse to initiate or change, the identification, evaluation, or educational placement of the child or the provision of an appropriate education. The schools also must convey the details of the proposed action and the reasons for the action.

Parents may request a due process hearing if they are not happy with any or all aspects of the procedures or the education of their child with a disability. The purpose of the due process hearing is to resolve differences of opinion between parents and school officials regarding the education, placement, or services for the child with a disability. If parents request a hearing, a hearing officer independent of the local education agency conducts the hearing. The hearing is at a time and place suitable to the parents.

A due process hearing tends to be an antagonistic process. It usually ends with both parties unhappy about the results or feeling they received less than they wanted. It is a legal procedure, and like other legal procedures, it has inherent problems. Due process hearings require an enormous amount of energy, time, and money. However, due process procedures are an invaluable means of ensuring an appropriate education and the participation of parents in the education of their children.

Instead of due process hearings, more individuals and school systems are using another form of resolution called mediation. Mediation involves the use of less formal, less adversarial, more negotiated-settlement meetings for resolving disputes. Usually in mediation, a neutral party hears the issues and helps to find an acceptable solution. There has been a significant increase in the number of cases using mediation.

Transition

Transition services are a coordinated set of activities for a student, designed within an outcome-oriented process, to promote movement from school to postschool activities. This includes postsecondary education, vocational training, integrated employment (including supported employment), continuing and adult education, adult services, independent living, and/or community. While early special education law provided access to school for students with disabilities, it did not consider issues of postschool life for these individuals.

In 1984, transition from school to work for students with disabilities became a major priority for the Office of Special Education and Rehabilitative Services (OSERS), raising the national profile of this issue. OSERS initiatives stressed that students with disabilities could potentially move into integrated employment in the community rather than simply into a sheltered workshop or work activity center.

Three main factors brought about the changes in transition services for students with disabilities: (a) the lessons of history, (b) the realization that students with disabilities were leaving a free appropriate public education and entering a system where there were no mandates, and (c) the fact that students educated in special education were not achieving desired outcomes.

THE REHABILITATION ACT OF 1973

Commonly referred to as the "Rehab Act" or "Section 504," this law authorizes payment of federal funds to institutions (or the withholding of those funds) based on compliance with regulations governing the education of students with disabilities. Section 504 of the Rehabilitation Act states that "No otherwise qualified individual with handicaps shall solely by reason of her or his handicap, be excluded from the participation in, be denied the benefits of, or be subjected to discrimination under any program or activity receiving Federal financial assistance" (29 U.S.C. § 794(a)).

This act protects from discrimination any person, including a student, whom the law considers as having a disability. Individuals must meet one of three criteria: "(i) has a physical or mental impairment which substantially limits one or more of such person's major life activities, (ii) has a record of such an impairment, or (iii) is regarded as having such an impairment" (29 U.S.C. § 706).

For the purposes of Section 504, "major life activities" include caring for one's self, performing manual tasks, walking, seeing, hearing, speaking, breathing, learning, and working. The law protects individuals from both intentional and unintentional discrimination. Under Section 504, individuals who have a disability might need assistance to qualify for the related services necessary for them to benefit from education. Section 504 also has provisions for nondiscriminatory employment.

The Section 504 definition for individuals with a disability and the descriptors of major life events are the same as the definitions used in the Americans With Disabilities Act (ADA).

THE AMERICANS WITH DISABILITIES ACT OF 1990

Though the Rehabilitation Act was passed in 1973, individuals with disabilities continued as a group to occupy an inferior status in our society, and were severely disadvantaged socially, vocationally, economically, and educationally. Congress strengthened the law through subsequent amendments and by the passage of the Americans With Disabilities Act (ADA) in 1990. The language of ADA is analogous to the language of the Rehab Act: "Subject to the provision of this title, no qualified individual with a disability, shall by reason of such disability, be excluded from participation in or be denied the benefits of services, programs, or activities of a public entity, or be subjected to discrimination by such entity" (ADA, Section 12132).

The Rehab Act and ADA impact the education of children with disabilities because they allow statutory venues for remediation of complaints. Individuals with disabilities and their families have an avenue through which they can file complaints against public schools. If their complaints are valid, a school's federal funds could be terminated. A typical example is a student with a physical disability who does not require special assistance for his education, and therefore is not classified as needing special education. However, he is still considered as having a disability under the three-part definition of Section 504 of the Rehab Act. Under Section 504, it would be illegal to discriminate against this child regarding activities, events, or classes. Section 504 of the Rehab Act and ADA are broader and more inclusive than the Individuals with Disabilities Education Act (IDEA).

The ADA strives for "equality of opportunity, full participation, independent living, and economic self-sufficiency" (42 U.S.C. 12101 et seq., § 2[a][8]) for persons with disabilities. The main purpose of the ADA is to provide civil rights to the 43 million Americans with disabilities who have been unable to access their communities and necessary services. Critics argue the ADA prevents businesses from expanding and wrecks small business. However, its main interest is to promote equal access and freedom for people with disabilities. Others state the ADA is an extension on the installment of a contract between individuals with disabilities, their family members, and the government for a lifetime of services and accessibility that starts with special education services received in schools. The intent of the ADA is to open more of society to people with disabilities. It is clear, however, that the ADA is changing the norms of society.

THE FAMILY EDUCATIONAL RIGHTS
AND PRIVACY ACT OF 1974

The Family Educational Rights and Privacy Act of 1974 (FERPA) does more than define who may and may not see student records;

⇒ FERPA guarantees the parents or guardians of a student to inspect and review their child's records.

⇒ FERPA establishes policies through which parents can challenge the accuracy of student records.

⇒ FERPA establishes a mechanism through which parents can appeal concerning alleged failures to comply with the law.

⇒ FERPA prohibits the release of information about a student without parent or guardian consent, except to those who have a legitimate right to know.

⇒ FERPA establishes that school districts need to have a written policy about who will have access to student records.

All of the information obtained as a part of the assessment process to determine whether a student has a disability must be included in the student's file. The only exceptions to this are the actual test protocols used by the individual administering the psychological and educational assessments. Additionally, student files should include evaluation reports, individualized education programs (IEPs), and summaries of progress toward IEP goals and objectives.

The substance of FERPA is that all of a student's records are located in the files, parents have access to them, they can challenge them, and the files contain confidential information. Knowing this, all school principals should be judicious about who has access. In addition, it is necessary to safeguard the files, and ensure appropriate information remains in the files.

NO CHILD LEFT BEHIND ACT

In 2001, Congress also passed the No Child Left Behind Act (NCLB). No Child Left Behind includes requirements about parental involvement, highly-qualified teachers, scientifically based reading instruction, tutoring and supplemental educational services, research-based teaching methods, and school and school district report cards. Chapter 4 contains full description of the law and what principals need to know.

4

The No Child Left Behind Act: What Do Principals Need to Know?

DOROTHY J. O'SHEA AND LAWRENCE J. O'SHEA

The No Child Left Behind Act (NCLB) of 2001 is a landmark educational reform bill designed to improve all student achievement. With the passage of NCLB, Congress reauthorized the Elementary and Secondary Education Act (ESEA) of 1965, the primary federal law that affects education from kindergarten through high school in America. NCLB requires states to implement statewide assessment systems aligned to state standards in increasing student performance and in boosting schools' overall effectiveness on student learning. What role do principals play in implementing NCLB mandates? What are their obligations and responsibilities regarding adequate yearly progress, and school improvement plans?

THE NCLB MANDATES

The Elementary and Secondary Education Act of 1965 (ESEA) initiated a number of programs that provided federal assistance to states in implementing educational programs for poor children. When Congress passed the ESEA, and with its reauthorization in 1994 (i.e., Improving America's Schools Act), there was a strong belief that federal influence would significantly change state and local policies and procedures by which schools educate our nation's children and youth. Continuing with the recent reauthorization of the ESEA, the intent of the 2002 passage of the No Child Left Behind Act (NCLB) was to enhance the federal government's commitment to ensuring equal access to education for poor and disadvantaged students, promote educational excellence for all of America's students, and hold schools accountable for the performance of their students. Accordingly, NCLB requires states to ensure that highly qualified teachers are in every classroom, using research-based practices as the foundation of their instruction. NCLB stresses the development of tests and/or alternative

The definition of the 2% rule is based on future federal guidance (see http://www.ed.gov/nclb/freedom/local/specedfactsheet.html). However, this 2% of the tested population is in addition to the 1% of the tested population whose scores on an alternative assessment may be counted toward proficiency. (The original NCLB mandated that the number of those proficient scores may not exceed 1% of all students in the grades tested, or about 9% of students with disabilities).

Students with severe cognitive disabilities are to be assessed by how well they achieve standards appropriate for their intellectual development, thus allowing states to more accurately gauge their progress. Examples of alternative assessment include the use of recording, observing, and monitoring behavior by faculty and staff familiar with students' classroom performances (such as through video recording or teleconferencing monitoring). The 2% rule is intended to address those special education "gap" students who perform below grade level, but are not considered to have significant cognitive disabilities that would allow them to take current statewide assessment. The provision for students with severe cognitive disabilities does not limit how many students can be tested with an alternate assessment; it limits only the number of scores *based on alternate achievement standards* that can be included as proficient in AYP measurement calculations.

Alternate achievement standards must be tied to state academic content standards, and allow states and school districts to exceed the 1% limit if they can demonstrate that they have a larger population of students with the most significant cognitive disabilities.

Individual schools are not subject to the 1% cap, as it applies only to district and state accountability decisions.

What Are Key Assessment Activities for Principals?

Students with special education needs must participate in required statewide assessment or alternative assessment procedures. Principals work collaboratively with stakeholders to locate, implement, and evaluate effective statewide assessment testing accommodations and modifications that will increase participation by students with diverse needs. An accommodation, which is defined as changes in the way a student is tested, does not change the intent of the test; it helps a student become successful in a particular subject by taking down those barriers a disability may bring to the table. When diverse learners such as students with disabilities traditionally participated in statewide assessment, they were often just given alternative assessment. The five most frequently allowed testing accommodations include the use of dictated response, large print, Braille, extended time, and sign language interpretation for instructions. Another popular accommodation included the use of reading aloud the test. The most controversial accommodations were the use of reading aloud the test, calculators, and scribing.

The scores of students with disabilities may be optimal, but optimal scores may not be valid indicators of a student's level of performance because they mask the true effects of the disability. In order to realize ongoing AYP, many students require changes either to the test format or how it is presented to get a true indication of what a student knows about a subject and what he or she can do. Accommodations in statewide assessment, such as increased time or the use of assistive technology, require further research study, to ensure that the unique needs of diverse learners are taken into account as they participate with their peers in the statewide assessment process to determine AYP.

Accommodations that benefit students with and without disabilities are of concern because when all students might benefit from an accommodation provided only to students with disabilities, the accommodation provides an unfair advantage to those with disabilities.

Consequences of Statewide Assessment for Students With Disabilities

NCLB builds on the 1997 amendments to the Individuals with Disabilities Education Act—which mandate that all students with disabilities must be tested—by ensuring that schools, districts, and states receive credit under AYP for students who are tested against different achievement standards. The amended NCLB provision was originally published in the Federal Register on March 20, 2005. A significant change from the proposed regulation is the elimination of a definition of students with significant cognitive disabilities. Rather, states will define this group of students.

Because the consequences of statewide assessment for students with disabilities are not clear, research-based practices espoused by concerned principals and their local stakeholders and state policymakers should include how to make standardized tests fair to all students, including students with disabilities, students from impoverished districts and families, those whose first language is not English, and minority students. Principals and local stakeholders should examine parental involvement in students' education as well as students' cultural opportunities, as both factors have shown to play a significant role in student achievement.

Maintaining appropriate or obtaining improved proficiency scores on statewide assessment remains a difficult task for principals charged with monitoring the delivery of effective, research-based instruction to all diverse learners. AYP stakes are high for diverse learners, as a failure to make proficient on statewide assessment may lock some students out of a regular diploma and the many benefits that accompany high school graduation. Principals working to ensure NCLB and the IDEA 2004 mandates are instrumental in bringing every public student up to state standards in achievement by 2014. Principals and stakeholders work to close the achievement gap based on culture, ethnicity, and language.

Principals work in their schools to show that the local site is working toward increasing AYP in making sure that all students achieve academic proficiency on state assessment.

Principals play an important liaison role with local stakeholders, district administrators, and state officials in securing, implementing, and accounting for appropriate levels of funding to design and implement annual tests for all students to let parents know the quality of the education their children are receiving. This is done regardless of race, income, or disability. Principals are key players in collecting data on local

TABLE 4-1. CONTRADICTIONS BETWEEN NCLB AND IDEA

NCLB	IDEA
Requires that all students progress at a similar rate.	Recognizes that all students progress at individual rates.
Uses standardized data sources to address progress.	Uses multiple data sources aligned to a student's abilities.
Uses chronological age and grade as a basis for state assessment.	Uses individualized assessment of a student's instructional level designated on his or her individualized education program (IEP).
Requires student progress to be determined by a "proficient" score on state tests.	Progress is based on an IEP team decision with test scores used as one contributing factor.

accountability that can have an impact on subject area achievement and school improvement results, including district attendance, enrollment, graduation requirements, and curriculum development.

RELATED AYP ELEMENTS AND THE PRINCIPAL'S ROLE

School Attendance

Local districts use data from each school to demonstrate year-to-year increases in school attendance. Principals work collaboratively with stakeholders to locate, implement, and evaluate effective attendance strategies that will maintain or increase AYP proficiency. Principals play key roles in helping their local schools to identify improvement targets for student attendance and to devise and reflect upon the school's core beliefs and mission. Principals lend a voice guiding what schools need to know and be able to do in order to support a student's desire to remain and succeed in school. Creating a *positive school climate* for all students is a must; this means ensuring that all students and families feel respected and welcome in the school, even if students come from outside the school's attendance zone or if they are participating in community-based programs. By respecting students' and families' cultural, ethnic, and language backgrounds through the promotion of home-school activities or community involvement in school functions, principals help to ensure that the school's environment encourages the participation and attendance of all learners.

Graduation Rates

Local districts use data from high schools to demonstrate year-to-year increases in 4-year graduation rates for high school students. Principals work collaboratively with stakeholders to locate, implement, and evaluate increased graduation rates and effective transition to adult programs that will maintain or increase AYP. Principals play key roles in helping their local school to *identify improvement targets* for diverse students who tend to drop out and who in the past have not made successful transitions to adult life. AYP "proficiency" for graduation and transition to adult life may take on different appearances for diverse learners. For example, strategies may focus on increased enrollments in institutions of higher education, services, or vocational sites for higher functioning students, while for more cognitively impaired students, transition activities may highlight planning future living arrangements, leisure-social activities, or sheltered workshop experiences. Frequent assessments of attendance and transition progress on meeting state standards and IEP transition goals are an important part of the educational process, excluding no student, even students with profound cognitive disabilities. Principals work to ensure that staff development and ongoing training efforts reflect the principles of effective transition goals for all learners.

LEGISLATIVE CONTRADICTIONS AND CONCERNS

Principals play a leadership role in local AYP practices and accountability to diverse learners, including students with disabilities. Principals must be strong advocates in helping their schools reach and maintain AYP, while ensuring all students are assessed accurately and receive opportunities to make learning progress. Principals reflect on AYP practices that work, based on external evidence and benchmarks of success across multiple classrooms and learning environments. However, in order to support appropriate AYP practices, each local principal must be knowledgeable about NCLB requirements and the overlap between these requirements and the 2004 IDEA requirements underscoring effective special education and related services practices. They must understand the differences between the NCLB and the IDEA mandates.

Contradictions Between NCLB and IDEA

The special education community has continuing concerns about ensuring that students with disabilities are expected to perform; however, practitioners are confused and concerned about the differences between the NCLB and the IDEA mandates. Those contradictions are shown in Table 4-1.

The Problem With Highly Qualified Teachers

Special educators are also concerned about the NCLB requirement for *highly qualified teachers*. Currently, NCLB requires that all teachers of core academic subjects be "highly qualified." This means that they demonstrate they have a college degree, have full certification or licensure, and have demonstrated competency in the subject(s) they teach. These criteria can be fulfilled by a college major in the subject, passing a state test, or demonstrating content knowledge through a state standard of evaluation. However, criteria completion is a major problem for special education teachers and programs. The content-area requirements are particularly burdensome to middle and high school special education teachers, who often work with students in several content areas. Many special education teachers will need to acquire additional content-area credentials in more than one subject, problematic in the field of special education, which is already suffering extreme shortages nationwide. Modifications of NCLB on these issues will most likely be provided in the IDEA regulations; however, principals hiring and retaining teaching faculty require flexible options that can support students, faculty, and staff, with an acute awareness of mandates to demonstrate AYP.

SCHOOL IMPROVEMENT PLANS

Effective school improvement plans result from effective collaboration and discussion and reflection among key stakeholders, and between local schools and communities. By facilitating concerted efforts toward ongoing school improvement, reflective principals help to ensure the alignment of stakeholders on common purposes—seeking and pursuing a common vision. Furthermore, principals help to align the school's needs and resources with its educational priorities. By voicing priorities and maintaining the data analysis process, principals help local stakeholders to be results-focused, and local schools become a community of learners reviewing, analyzing, and reflecting on data-based decision making as they seek to institutionalize student achievement and educational practices.

The Principal's Role in School Improvement Plans

Key activities in school improvement plans integrate a principal's roles in school organization, leadership, curriculum and instruction, staff development, school climate, and assessment.

Principals spend time observing in classrooms to monitor educational practices and to provide immediate feedback to faculty and staff. Principals seeking to increase school improvement elicit input from all sources to improve student achievement. They involve all school staff in some fashion, and solicit input from parents, students, and other stakeholders, ensuring that all voices are heard. However, principals also assume frequent monitoring roles and directly and explicitly observe faculty and staff, providing immediate and ongoing feedback concerning performance.

Principals seeking to increase school improvement gains remain data-driven; response to effective intervention is an ongoing process. Principals obtain, use, evaluate, and reflect on data concerning student achievement and other evidence about the quality and effectiveness of local practices. Ongoing data collection and analysis inform principals' discussions with local stakeholders and state or federal officials when determining effectiveness of school improvement plans. As such, principals help faculty and staff to collect data that can be disaggregated, underscoring results related to specific state standards or AYP objectives. They help faculty and staff build expertise in data analysis, providing adequate time for faculty and staff to respond and allowing faculty and staff to adopt changes in curriculum and instruction that address needs identified from data analysis.

Principals seeking to increase school improvement gains provide the means for faculty and staff to use evidence-based practices. Such principals search for information about proven practices and research-based approaches, and visit, observe, and reflect on similar schools that are getting good results. They ensure that data on special education and related services are available and accessible to faculty and staff, and encourage school personnel to take advantage of that material. Principals encourage faculty and staff to take part in current training and professional development that will expand and enhance their skills in and knowledge of working with diverse learners, and to become active members of professional associations concerned with the education of diverse learners. Because they allow time for school and community professionals, as well as parents to participate in school functions, community activities, or professional development, principals enhance school-home-community relationships.

Principals work on an ongoing bases with local stakeholders to document long-range priorities. Principals identify primary priorities which they can implement successfully and which will produce high-impact results. By analyzing and reflecting on collected data, they work with local school boards to ensure that school improvement plans contain sound educational practices that have a high likelihood of successful implementation and student and school performance improvement. When implemented, observations of local school plans have a high probability of improving student achievement and meeting district improvement targets. Principals put forth effective improvement targets that focus on aligning local resources (staff, budget, etc.) with identified local needs, as principals attend to careful implementation, follow-through, and continuous evidence-based monitoring of progress. They accomplish desired local results at the grass-roots level where students are served, as is the intention of the NCLB mandates.

FINAL THOUGHTS

Principals facilitate the process to meet the NCLB mandates by articulating supports and services available in local areas. They help to monitor local roles and responsibilities of school and district personnel. Effective principals elicit training, support, and accountability mechanisms through collaboration efforts with local stakeholders. Because they are key players in quality reviews of their local plans, and they seek AYP, principals help to imbue a sense of commitment, accountability, and caring as schools and students improve. As such, principals are necessary to federal mandate success.

5

What Does a Principal Need to Know About Determining Special Education Eligibility?

Susan Gilmartin Foltz and Johanna Rich Tesman

Before students can receive special education or related services, they need to be assessed and identified as eligible to receive these services. The Individuals with Disabilities Education Improvement Act of 2004 provides specific guidelines to ensure that children are appropriately assessed, requiring that a "team of qualified professionals" (including parents) determine eligibility for special education and related services. The principal's role in the process from prereferral to assessment is multifaceted, ensuring the school follows appropriate procedures and timelines, while working to meet the needs of the student in the classroom. If there are problems in the procedures used in determining a child's eligibility, this calls into question every aspect of the services provided to the student.

FIRST STEPS

Some children, because of severe or obvious disability, participate in early intervention programs as infants or toddlers. These children have already gone through the assessment process, been found eligible, and receive services to facilitate their development. (If a school-age child is already identified, follow the monitoring and reevaluation procedures discussed below.)

For most children, the process of determining eligibility begins in the general education classroom. The teacher notices that something is "different" about this child, either academically or behaviorally. The student might have difficulty performing at grade level, paying attention, following directions, getting along with others, or using fine or gross motor skills.

Identifying a student with difficulties in the classroom does not automatically correlate to eligibility for special education. In fact, many problems that students exhibit in the general education classroom can be handled there without assistance, through classroom modifications and accommodations. Perhaps the student needs to be seated closer to the board or to the teacher, or needs help with organizing his personal space (desk, locker, or cubbyhole.) Whatever problem the student exhibits, the first step is to try to ameliorate the problem while maintaining the student in his or her classroom. This is called *prereferral intervention.*

Prereferral Intervention

The purpose of prereferral intervention is to find ways to increase the student's success in the general education classroom without special education or related services. The prereferral intervention stage requires that general education teachers be able to address the increasing variability in the learning characteristics of the students they teach. This process includes identifying the student's academic or behavioral needs, modifying the curriculum and/or the environment, and monitoring student progress. Prereferral interventions can be very informal, requiring relatively minor modifications or instructional adaptations, and special education services are never needed. In every case where a school screens a student's needs and implements prereferral interventions, however, it must collect data on the success or failure of the interventions. This data will help determine if further interventions are needed. If the data determine that the student is now successful, further interventions are not needed and the student continues in the general education class. If the data suggest that further interventions are needed, then the referral process begins. There are some students for whom simpler classroom modifications are not sufficient.

During the prereferral process, after the classroom teacher has noticed that a student is demonstrating academic or behavior problems, all observations and and modifications must be documented. The teacher should document everything that demonstrates the extent of the problem(s) and the attempts made to effect change. The teacher should provide examples of the work that differentiates the student from the class. Also, it may be appropriate to ask the teacher to provide examples of behavior and when and where it is demonstrated, or time samples of off-task behavior. This is where it may be important for the principal, the guidance counselor, or the school psychologist to offer assistance. The principal (or the aforementioned personnel) may want to observe and make recommendations about how to respond to the student's behaviors. A detailed description of the problem from the teacher combined with an observation by another professional may help to further define the problem and/or assist in formulating recommendations.

It can be helpful to use a systematic observation system such as Edward Shapiro's (2004a and 2004b) Behavioral Observation of Students in Schools system (BOSS), or the Behavior Assessment for Children (BASC) Student Observation System (SOS) (Reynolds & Kamphaus, 2004). Behavioral rating systems allow one to compare the behavior of the student in question with a peer match. This comparison process allows you to describe the actions of the child and others in the classroom so that there is as little room for interpretation as possible. It is important to compare the student to others in the class. Perhaps a student is only on task 50% of the time; this might seem like an important piece of information and might indicate that the student is having problems. However, if other students in the class are only on task 30-40% of the time, the student who is on task 50% of the time is not atypical.

It is important to note that prereferral is only the first step in acquiring assistance for a student. The use of prereferral interventions cannot deny the services that a student may need by delaying the assessment process. If more intensive interventions seem needed, the principal should seek parental permission for evaluation.

Response to Intervention

IDEA 2004 modified the definition of *learning disability*. Rather than only looking at a severe discrepancy between achievement and intellectual ability (the traditional IQ-achievement discrepancy model), the local educational agency (i.e., someone at the child's school) can use a process that determines if the child responds to scientific, research-based intervention. According to IDEA 2004, a student *cannot* be determined to have a disability if the determining factor is (a) a lack of scientifically-based instructional practices and programs that contain the essential components of reading instruction, (b) a lack of instruction in math, or (c) limited English proficiency. IDEA 2004 changes and the No Child Left Behind Act have in turn initiated changes in the prereferral process in some states; most states have specific procedures for prereferral intervention. This overall process is often generally referred to as Response to Intervention (RTI). In the RTI model, evaluation and intervention are essentially conducted concurrently; students progress through several levels of intervention before entering special education. Proponents of the RTI model argue that the traditional discrepancy model does not provide a direct link to intervention, that there can be both false positives and false negatives with IQ and achievement testing, and that the model basically takes a "wait-to-fail" approach.

The RTI model (see Figure 5-1) has at its basis a three-tiered decision-making process that has primarily been applied to reading instruction. In this model, tier one is screening and intervention, for example, an early literacy program that is applied to all students and has both an instructional and a screening component. Tier two is assessing response to instruction during team-based problem-solving (e.g., RTI). Tier three is appraising the extent of academic problems and evaluating the need for specially designed instruction—that is, special education services.

The RTI process identifies students who have not been making expected progress in the general education curriculum and are considered to be at risk for academic failure; for example, a student who is not learning to read in kindergarten would be considered not to be making progress. Once a student has been identified as being at risk, long- and short-term goals are set for that student's progress in order to establish benchmarks and standards. Academic interventions are adjusted frequently. The critical components of RTI are:

⟶ Universal screening of academic functioning.

⟶ A three-tiered intervention model.

⟶ Differentially tiered intervention strategy.

⟶ Making use of evidence-based interventions.

⟶ Continuous monitoring of student performance.

⟶ Benchmark/outcome assessment.

REFERRAL

If the student still does not make progress after various observations, modifications, and interventions, the teachers, educational specialist, school counselor, administrator, or parents can initiate the referral process. As noted above, the prereferral process should not delay a referral. Within 10 days of referral initiation—even if you are working to implement prereferral interventions—you need to make a determination about whether further evaluation is necessary.

A referral should document the reasons why the child should be tested for special education eligibility. It should give some indication of the problem areas of the student. Most districts have formal referral forms for teachers and administrators to use, which include such essential information as

✓ The student's name.

✓ Age of student.

✓ Grade level of student.

✓ Name of person initiating the referral.

✓ Relationship to the student.

✓ Problems manifested in the classroom.

✓ Steps taken to relieve the problem.

✓ Outcome(s) of those steps.

✓ The date the referral was initiated.

It would be nice to have the same supporting documentation when the referral is initiated by the parent; however, they just need to put in writing that they want the child tested. As a principal and a member of the multidisciplinary team, you can gather the information from the other members of the team to determine if testing is warranted.

INITIAL MULTIDISCIPLINARY TEAM MEETING

The initial multidisciplinary team meeting is held to determine if the child warrants testing. Under IDEA 2004, the team can choose not to evaluate the child if they feel there is no basis to suspect that there is a disability. For example, psychological evaluations may not be appropriate because of issues such as social service and postsecondary eligibility and issues related to retention and promotion. If parents initiate a referral for testing and the team decides testing is not necessary, the parents need to be notified in writing. At that same time, they need to be notified of their due process rights (see Chapter 9 for more information).

FIGURE 5-1. RTI MODEL

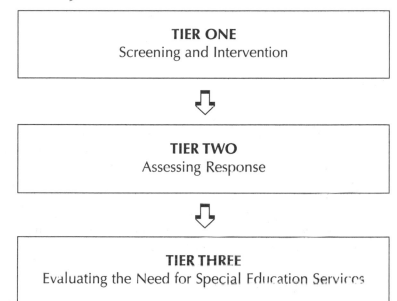

The team should consist of the general education teacher; an individual knowledgeable about the suspected disability; the parent(s); and an administrator, such as the principal, who knows the student, and knows how the student is functioning compared to other students in the school. Someone at the meeting should take notes and keep track of any documentation.

 The meeting notes should describe what occurred at the meeting, and include the team's specific recommendations.

Before the meeting collect

✓ Examples of class work from the student, and from "typical" students.

✓ Notes from observations.

✓ Results from screening instruments or normative tests.

✓ Comments from previous teachers.

✓ Copies of report cards.

✓ Comments from others who may be involved with the student (e.g., the art teacher, music teacher, librarian, or physical education teacher).

✓ Any notes on behaviors (positive and negative) that you have kept on the student.

All meeting participants should have material indicating the student's name, age, and grade level; name of person initiating the referral and relationship to the student; and problems manifested in the classroom, steps taken to relieve the problem, and outcome(s) of those steps, and whether the student has been retained. If the parent made the referral and is not in attendance, the child's teacher(s) should describe the academic and social behavior of the student in question and present information on how this student compares to others in the class.

At the meeting

1.   Call the meeting to order.

2.   State that you are gathered to determine if the student needs testing to see if they are eligible for special education.

3.   State that the purpose of the meeting is not to determine who will be providing services to the student, but to determine whether testing is warranted to determine if the student needs special education.

4.   The individual who made the referral should present information about the student.

5.   Ask for comments and questions, discussing the salient points of the presentation.

6.   Ask for a recommendation from one of the team members.

7.   Discuss the recommendation, working to come to consensus as a team.

8.   If necessary, vote on the recommendation.

If the team recommends testing the child for special education services, the team should specify the particular areas of concern. For example, the child might have problems reading, or have problems in organization and impulse control, or have problems with peer and social relations. Whatever information the team can provide that will assist the individuals who are doing the testing will help the child.

If the team does not recommend testing for special education at this time, describe why you do not think the student needs testing. The team members should make recommendations to the teacher that can help improve the student's performance.

The parents, the child's permanent file, and the individual in your district responsible for coordinating testing all need a written copy of the results of the meeting, including information on the team's recommendation as to whether the child should be tested, and any additional recommendations on specific areas of assessment. The written record should include the team members' names and signatures.

PARENTAL NOTIFICATION AND CONSENT

If the multidisciplinary team recommends testing the child to determine eligibility for special education, the next step is to obtain parental consent. The district administrators must notify the parents in writing of their intent to assess the child for special education and the reasons for the assessment. Parents must be provided with a written statement of their rights under the law; this statement needs to be understandable to the public. Parents need to be apprised of their due process rights. They also need an explanation of the tests, who will be doing the testing, when the tests will occur, and how long the process will take. Finally, the parents need to be aware of what the likely results will be if their child is found eligible for special education. The parents then sign a paper stating they have received their notice of rights.

For testing to occur, the parents need to provide consent. If the parents do not provide consent for an evaluation, or the parent fails to respond to a request to provide consent, due process hearing procedures may be used to obtain authority for the evaluation.

THE EVALUATION

Federal regulations are very prescriptive about what needs to be included in an evaluation for special education. Principals need to understand the procedures helping order to effectively monitor it, and to help answer questions about the appropriateness or the stage of the process.

This section discusses federal regulations in 34 C.F.R. § 300.301-311 regarding the assessment of individuals for special education; state regulations vary, but all must satisfy the federal regulations.

Assessment Tools

There are a variety of assessment tools and strategies used to gather relevant functional and developmental information about a student. No single procedure is to be used as the sole criteria for determining whether a child has an eligible disability or for determining an appropriate educational program for the child.

The selected assessment tools and strategies must provide relevant information that directly assists in determining the educational needs of the child.

The student must be assessed in all areas related to the suspected disability including, as appropriate, health, vision, hearing, social and emotional status, general intelligence, academic performance, communicative status, and motor abilities. Technically sound instruments are to be used to assess the relative contribution of cognitive and behavioral factors, in addition to physical or developmental factors. The evaluation must be sufficiently comprehensive as to identify all of the child's special education and related services needs, whether or not commonly linked to the disability category in which the child might be classified.

Because the assessment process for the student needs to be individualized, based on the referral, a standardized assessment provided to every child suspected of having a disability violates the spirit of the law, and does not work to assess what a specific child might need. All assessments need to be individualized; do not use a group-administered test to determine whether a child has a disability. Use a group-administered test to "screen" for a disability, but not for a disability determination.

Selected tests cannot be discriminatory on a racial or cultural basis; and must be provided and administered in the child's native language or other mode of communication, unless it is clearly not feasible to do so. In selecting tests to assess a child with limited English proficiency, ensure that they measure the extent to which the child has a disability and needs special education, rather than measuring the child's English language skills. If a test is administered to a child with impaired sensory, manual, or speaking skills, the results should accurately reflect the child's aptitude or achievement level or whatever other factors the test purports to measure, rather than reflecting the child's impaired sensory, manual, or speaking skills (unless those skills are the factors that the test purports to measure).

Rating scales help to assess the presence or frequency of certain behaviors or skills and are often completed by those who are very familiar with the student, such as parents and teachers. Typically, rating scales are normed to particular populations to assist in the determination of whether behaviors are "typical" or significantly different from peers. Rating scales can be broadband measures such as BASC (Reynolds & Kamphaus, 2004), in which a range of externalizing and internalizing behaviors are looked at, or they can be behavior-specific. (For example, the Conners Rating Scale-R (CRS-R) (1997) is typically used to help in the diagnosis of attention deficit/hyperactivity disorder).

School-aged children who are competent readers (typically age 7 and above) can complete *self-report* measures in order to get a systematic report of internal state. For example, the Beck Depression Inventory (1996) can be used to help identify depressive symptoms.

Observations by a psychologist or other educational professional can give an indication of how the student is functioning in his or her academic environment and how others are interacting with him or her. For example, in the case of autistic students it can be extremely informative to evaluate them in unstructured times such as recess, lunch, and transitioning from one class to another.

Interviewing students can help in gathering information regarding interpersonal relationships, history, and prominent concerns. Similarly, interviewing parents and teachers allows one to gather critical information regarding medical, developmental, and educational history.

Standardized Tests

Standardized tests allow one to compare a student's performance to that of an appropriate peer group. These tests are normed under standardized conditions to ensure that one is able to make reliable and valid comparisons. For example, two gold standards of intelligence testing are the Wechsler Intelligence Scale for Children (WISC) and the Stanford Binet.

The selected standardized tests must have been validated for the specific purpose for which they are used and are to be administered by trained and knowledgeable personnel in accordance with instructions provided by the producer of the tests. If an assessment is not conducted under standard conditions, the evaluation report must include a description of the extent to which it varied from standard conditions (e.g., the qualifications of the person administering the test, or the method of test administration).

Tests and other evaluation materials must be tailored to assess the specific areas of educational need.

Psychological Assessment

The National Association of School Psychologists (2003) describes psychological evaluations as a "set of assessment procedures administered by a licensed psychologist or credentialed school psychologist to obtain information about a student's learning, behavior, or mental health (NASP, 2003)." They note that evaluations are conducted for determining eligibility but also done to develop behavioral and instructional interventions, identify mental health disorders, and identify giftedness and school readiness; the selection of assessment procedure or combination of procedures should be based on the reasons for referral.

SPECIFIC GUIDELINES FOR DETERMINING ELIGIBILITY FOR LEARNING DISABILITIES

Specific guidelines for determining that a child is eligible for the category of specific learning disability are included to facilitate your work with the largest category in special education.

Criteria for Determining the Existence of a Specific Learning Disability

(a) A team may determine that a child has a specific learning disability if

   (1) The child does not achieve commensurate with his or her age and ability levels in one or more of the areas listed if provided with learning experiences appropriate for the child's age and ability levels.

   (2) The team finds that a child has a severe discrepancy between achievement and intellectual ability in one or more of the following areas:
      (i)   Oral expression.
      (ii)   Listening comprehension.
      (iii) Written expression.
      (iv)   Basic reading skill.
      (v)   Reading comprehension.
      (vi)   Mathematics calculation.
      (vii) Mathematics reasoning.

   (3) The team may not identify a child as having a specific learning disability if the severe discrepancy between ability and achievement is primarily the result of
      (i)   A visual, hearing, or motor impairment.
      (ii)   Mental retardation.
      (iii) Emotional disturbance.
      (iv)   Environmental, cultural, or economic disadvantage.

Written Report

A written report needs to be produced when a child is identified as having a specific learning disability.

   For a child suspected of having a specific learning disability, the documentation of the team's determination of eligibility, must include a statement of

(1) Whether the child has a specific learning disability.

(2) The basis for making the determination.

(3) The relevant behavior noted during the observation of the child.

(4) The relationship of that behavior to the child's academic functioning.

(5) The educationally relevant medical findings, if any.

(6) Whether there is a severe discrepancy between achievement and ability that is not correctable without special education and related services.

(7) The determination of the team concerning the effects of environmental, cultural, or economic disadvantage.

(b) Each team member shall certify in writing whether the report reflects his or her conclusion. If it does not reflect his or her conclusion, the team member must submit a separate statement presenting his or her conclusions.

Summary of Procedures

It is important to note the assessment must include all areas related to the suspected disability, and that the evaluation is comprehensive enough to identify all needed special education and related services. The time that the referral is initiated to the time that a meeting is held to determine whether a child is eligible for special education is prescribed by federal and state law. IDEA establishes a 60-day timeline from receipt of parent consent for evaluation.

SECTION 504 EVALUATIONS

There are subtle differences in the evaluative procedures for students qualifying for support under Section 504 of the Rehabilitation Act (see Chapter 3) and those of IDEA. It is important for principals to have a thorough understanding of the differences, because the principal is often responsible for ensuring the student with a disability is having his or her needs met under Section 504. IDEA 2004 requires a student to have a disability and need specially designed instruction. Section 504 only requires a student to have a disability.

Like IDEA, Section 504 regulations require that tests and all evaluation materials must be validated for the specific purpose for which they are used and administered by trained personnel in conformity with instructions provided by their producer. Assessment tools must be tailored to assess specific areas of educational need, and not merely provide a single intelligence quotient; and must be selected and administered so as to best ensure that the test results accurately reflect the student's aptitude or achievement level or whatever other factor the test purports to measure. For Section 504 assessments, the district must convene a group of persons knowledgeable about the student who understand the data from the tests and can make appropriate decisions about the placement of the student. Also, similar to IDEA, the parents have the right to be notified of their rights and file a grievance; to notification when eligibility is determined; to an evaluation that uses multiple sources; and to periodic reevaluation, and representation by counsel when needed.

INDEPENDENT EVALUATION

If the parents do not feel the evaluation of their child is adequate, they can request an independent educational evaluation by a qualified individual not affiliated with the district, at public expense. The independent evaluation can cover the territory covered by the other evaluation, or it can cover only part, such as diagnostic information about reading, or a different intelligence test.

When a parent requests an independent educational evaluation, the district has to provide a list of qualified individuals who provide evaluations.

A parent can request an independent educational evaluation at any time in the process, not just at the end after the evaluation results are presented.

The district must consider the results of the independent evaluation as a part of its decision making, though it does not have to accept the results as the definitive statement of the child's educational performance.

If the district does not accept the results of the independent evaluation, it must state the following in writing: a description of how the independent evaluation was made available to the district, a record of the subsequent discussion, and reasons for the disagreement.

A district does not have to grant the parent's request for an independent educational evaluation at public expense if it believes that its evaluation was appropriate. If the parents disagree with the district about whether the evaluation was appropriate, the parents have the right to request a due process hearing. If a due process hearing officer deems an independent evaluation is necessary, then the district should arrange for an independent evaluation as soon as possible.

If the due process hearing officer does not state that an independent educational evaluation is necessary, the parents still have the right to obtain an independent educational evaluation at their own expense. In fact, the parents may obtain as many independent educational evaluations at their expense as they want. The process for reviewing information when a parent pays for an independent evaluation is the same as when the district pays for the evaluation. The team needs to meet on the results, consider them, and then if they are not used, it should state why.

A final note on independent evaluations: The ultimate goal in obtaining an evaluation of a child is to assist in planning appropriate instruction. The team should consider the parents' request for an independent evaluation very carefully, keeping in mind the rationale behind the request. When results from the independent evaluation are presented, regardless of who might have done the assessments, review them in light of decisions about improving the education of the child.

EVALUATION FOR RELATED SERVICES

A main part of IDEA 2004 is that students who need special education often need related services in order for them to receive the benefits of education. If you suspect the child needs related services based upon the initial referral, then the student needs to be evaluated by individuals trained in the appropriate techniques. For example, if you suspect that the child needs physical therapy in addition to special education services for a specified disability, then a trained physical therapist needs to assess the child. All assessments for related services (such as occupational therapy, speech and language services, and counseling services) have to occur within the same period as the other assessments.

THE MULTIDISCIPLINARY TEAM MEETING

After you gather the information from the assessments, the multidisciplinary team needs to meet to review the results. Often principals lead the team meetings. Therefore, it is important for you to understand the roles of different members, the information expected from them, and the result of the meeting.

Scheduling the Meeting

✓ The meeting typically has to occur within 60 days after the initiation of the referral; state regulations delineate the timetable for review.

✓ Ensure that all participants can attend, such as the person who made the referral, the individuals who did the testing, the classroom teacher, and someone knowledgeable of the suspected disability.

✓ The meeting time should be convenient for the parent(s). You want them to be as informed about the decisions as possible.

✓ The meeting location should be as comfortable, quiet, and distraction-free as possible.

✓ Schedule about 2 hours for the meeting.

✓ If you hold the meeting during the school day, either hire a substitute teacher for the classroom teacher(s), or otherwise ensure that their classes are covered.

Before the Meeting

✓ Make sure that all the assessments are complete, and there are summaries for the results.

✓ Talk with the individuals who did the assessments seeking a quick summary of their results. You want to make sure additional testing is not necessary. If it is necessary, work to get it done before the meeting.

✓ Make sure that everyone knows about the date, time, purpose, and location of the meeting.

✓ Make sure that everyone will attend. If they are not going to attend, make the determination about whether you need to reschedule. However, you still need to keep the meeting within the timeframes as delineated by your state.

If you are not going to reschedule, obtain a copy and summary of the person's report so you can present the information to others. Determine who would be a suitable person to present the information, talk with them about it before you go into the meeting so they have a chance to review the report and ask questions of the author, if necessary.

✓ Designate someone who will be responsible for taking notes at the meeting.

✓ Let the office staff know where you will be, and that you are not to be interrupted. Also, let the office staff know there might be individuals not familiar with the school who will be attending the meeting. Tell the staff to look for them, and direct them to the right place.

Meeting Procedures

Remember that many parents feel overwhelmed by these meetings, especially because professionals present detailed information about their child. If you use acronyms or abbreviations to describe either the tests or the student, explain these terms to the parents so they are informed. You do not want them to feel the "professionals" are trying to talk over their head. Parents may need additional clarification about observations and assessment data, especially what the results mean for their child.

1. Thank everyone for coming. Explain to them that you are gathered to review assessment information to determine if a student is eligible for special education. Explain that you will be discussing detailed and very personal information about the student. Therefore, it is expected that all participants will discuss this confidential information with only those individuals who need to know.

2. Pass out a sign-up sheet for attendance purposes for individuals to list their names and titles or relationship to the student. Attendees should introduce themselves, explaining their position in the school.

3. Lay some ground rules: Explain that everyone will have opportunity to ask questions after each report, but should not interrupt the others while they are presenting their information. Explain that after the presentation of the reports, the team will make a decision about whether this child is eligible for special education. Explain that the purpose of this meeting is not to describe whom the student's teachers will be, or what subjects the student will be studying. That comes later, if the student is eligible, at the meeting to develop the student's individualized education program (IEP).

4. Review the process so far: Ask the person who initiated the referral to describe the problems the student was having and why they thought testing should occur. Have the person who observed the child state her or his observations, and have the others in attendance state the results of their assessments. Have the participants describe the child and the strengths the child has. The parents will appreciate this, and it will keep everyone focused on the real reason for the meeting: working to improve the education for this child. Review information from those not in attendance. Ask for comments and questions.

5. Read the definition of the suspected disability. You might need to read more than one definition. For example, if you are unsure if a child with a behavior

problem is eligible under the category of learning disability or the category of emotionally disturbed, read both. (See the definitions of different eligibility categories, below.)

6. There are several different recommendations that the team can make. It can recommend that the child is eligible for special education. It can recommend that the child is not eligible for special education. Alternatively, it can recommend a decision be deferred on this child because additional information is necessary, or some major life event occurred necessitating a waiting period (e.g., mother is very sick). The team needs to document the reason for the wait, obtain approval from the parent(s), and set a specific deadline for reconvening the meeting. This waiting period should be brief, for a specific function, and should not be used to delay services.

7. Ask for a discussion of the recommendation(s) or questions about the definition(s). After the discussion, the team needs to vote or otherwise indicate approval or disapproval of the recommendation. If there are team members who are opposed to the decision, they must be allowed to file a minority report.

8. Ask the parents if they have any questions about the process. Tell the parents they have a right to file a due process at any time if they are unhappy with the outcome of the meeting or the educational services provided to their child.

9. Thank the participants for their attendance and for their contributions. Remind the participants the information discussed at the meeting is confidential. Adjourn the meeting.

After the Meeting

1. As soon as possible, review the notes to make sure they accurately reflect what occurred. Copies of the notes need to be added to the child's permanent file, and sent to the director of special education or director of pupil personnel services.

2. Prepare the evaluation report (see below).

3. If the child is eligible for special education, a team must develop the IEP within the next 10 days.

4. If the child is not eligible, meet with the teacher to discuss strategies for this student, regardless of the problems discussed in the meeting.

5. Be available to meet with the parents to review the meeting. If you are not able to answer their questions, do not just refer them on. Take time to get the answers, making sure the parents know the results. It will take time, but the parents will benefit, and you will have a better understanding of the process and will be able to assist other parents in the future.

EVALUATION REPORT

After the multidisciplinary meeting determining the child's eligibility, regardless of the decision reached, a written report summarizes the information. The assessment process should have looked at the issue(s) raised about the child during the initial referral. Therefore, there should be a close tie between the initial referral and the summary of the tests in the comprehensive evaluation report.

➡ If the child is not found eligible, the report must include the findings from the meeting; test scores, summaries, and notes from observations; and suggestions for ways of improving service.

➡ If the child is determined to be eligible for special education, the report should specify the disability; describe the child's strengths and weaknesses; list the broad goals toward which the child should be working; and include scores and summaries, notes from observations, and a minority report if there was not unanimity. This report will provide the basis of the student's IEP. For more information see Chapter 6.

TRIENNIAL REEVALUATION

The complete assessment process reoccurs for each child in special education at least once every 3 years. This is the triennial evaluation. This determines if the student is still eligible; makes sure special education does not become the educational placement for those who do not need it; and adapts to a student's changing educational, social, and behavioral needs.

The big difference between the student's initial evaluation and the triennial reevaluation, is that the child does not have to go through the same complete battery of tests they went through the first time. As long as the reevaluation addresses the student's current needs, it does not have to be identical. The reevaluation should be similar to the original placement evaluation.

The term *triennial* describes the need for the evaluation to occur at least once every 3 years. If the child is making progress or the program does not seem to fit based on the previous evaluation, then do evaluations that are more frequent.

DISABILITY CATEGORIES

For a child to receive services in special education under IDEA, he or she must meet at least one of the categorical definitions. Your state may have a different definition than the ones the federal government uses; however, these serve as at least a benchmark from which to compare. These are the definitions used as a part of the multidisciplinary team decision.

General Definition of Disability

The term *child with a disability* (Sec. 300.8) means a child who is evaluated properly and who has mental retardation, a hearing impairment including deafness, a speech or language impairment, a visual impairment including blindness, serious emotional disturbance (hereafter referred to as emotional disturbance), an orthopedic impairment, autism, traumatic brain injury, another health impairment, a specific learning disability, deaf-blindness, or multiple disabilities, and who, by reason thereof, needs special education and related services.

Definition of Developmental Delay

The term *developmental delay* may be used to describe a disability for a child aged 3 through 9, who is experiencing developmental delays, as defined by the state and as measured by appropriate diagnostic instruments and procedures, in one or more of the following areas: physical development, cognitive development, communication development, social or emotional development, or adaptive development, and who, by reason thereof, needs special education and related services.

Autism

Autism is a developmental disability significantly affecting verbal and nonverbal communication and social interaction, generally evident before age 3, that adversely affects a child's educational performance. Other characteristics often associated with autism are engagement in repetitive activities and stereotyped movements, resistance to environmental change or change in daily routines, and unusual responses to sensory experiences. The term does not apply if a child's educational performance is adversely affected primarily because the child has an emotional disturbance.

Deaf-Blindness

Deaf-blindness identifies concomitant hearing and visual impairments, the combination of which causes such severe communication and other developmental and educational needs that they cannot be accommodated in special education programs solely for children with deafness or children with blindness.

Deafness

Deafness is a hearing impairment that is so severe that the child is impaired in processing linguistic information through hearing, with or without amplification, and the educational performance is adversely affected.

Emotional Disturbance

Emotional disturbance is a term that identifies a condition exhibiting one or more of the following characteristics over a long period of time and to a marked degree that adversely affects a child's educational performance:

- An inability to learn that cannot be explained by intellectual, sensory, or health factors.
- An inability to build or maintain satisfactory interpersonal relationships with peers and teachers.
- Inappropriate types of behavior or feelings under normal circumstances.
- A general pervasive mood of unhappiness or depression.
- A tendency to develop physical symptoms or fears associated with personal or school problems.

The term includes schizophrenia. The term does not apply to children who are socially maladjusted, unless it is determined that they have an emotional disturbance.

Hearing Impairment

Hearing impairment refers to an impairment in hearing, whether permanent or fluctuating, that adversely affects a child's educational performance, but that is not included under the definition of deafness in this section.

Mental Retardation

Mental retardation identifies significantly subaverage general intellectual functioning, existing concurrently with deficits in adaptive behavior and manifested during the developmental period, that adversely affects a child's educational performance.

Multiple Disabilities

Multiple disabilities means concomitant impairments (such as mental retardation-blindness, mental retardation-orthopedic impairment, etc.), the combination of which causes such severe educational needs that they cannot be accommodated in special education programs solely for one of the impairments. The term does not include deaf-blindness.

Orthopedic Impairment

Orthopedic impairment is a severe orthopedic impairment that adversely affects a child's educational performance. The term includes impairments caused by congenital anomaly (e.g., clubfoot, absence of some member, etc.), impairments caused by disease (e.g., poliomyelitis, bone tuberculosis, etc.), and impairments from other causes (e.g., cerebral palsy, amputations, and fractures or burns that cause contractures).

Other Health Impairment

Other health impairment means having limited strength, vitality or alertness, including a heightened alertness to environmental stimuli, that results in limited alertness with respect to the educational environment, that

- Is due to chronic or acute health problems such as asthma, attention deficit disorder or attention deficit/hyperactivity disorder, diabetes, epilepsy, a heart condition, hemophilia, lead poisoning, leukemia, nephritis, rheumatic fever, and sickle cell anemia.
- Adversely affects a child's educational performance.

Specific Learning Disability

Specific learning disability identifies a disorder in one or more of the basic psychological processes involved in understanding or in using language, spoken or written, that may manifest itself in an imperfect ability to listen, think, speak, read, write, spell, or to do mathematical calculations, including conditions such as perceptual disabilities, brain injury, minimal brain dysfunction, dyslexia, and developmental aphasia. The term does not include learning problems that are primarily the result of visual, hearing, or motor disabilities; of mental retardation; of emotional disturbance; or of environmental, cultural, or economic disadvantage.

Speech or Language Impairment

Speech or language impairment refers to communication disorders, such as stuttering, impaired articulation, or a language or voice impairment that adversely affect a child's educational performance.

Traumatic Brain Injury

Traumatic brain injury is an acquired injury to the brain caused by an external physical force, resulting in total or partial functional disability or psychosocial impairment, or both, that adversely affects a child's educational performance. The term applies to open or closed head injuries resulting in impairments in one or more areas, such as cognition; language; memory; attention; reasoning; abstract thinking; judgment; problem-solving; sensory, perceptual, and motor abilities; psychosocial behavior; physical functions; information processing; and speech. The term does not apply to brain injuries that are congenital or degenerative, or to brain injuries induced by birth trauma.

Visual Impairment

Visual impairment is an impairment in vision that, even with correction, adversely affects a child's educational performance. The term includes both partial sight and blindness.

Attention Deficit/Hyperactivity Disorder or ADHD

Attention deficit/hyperactivity disorder is included under the "other health impaired" definition. There is no specific category of ADD/ADHD, but this does not mean that students with ADD/ADHD do not get services. This has been considered a disability under Section 504.

The draft IDEA 2004 regulations amend the definition of "other health impairment" to add ADD/ADHD to the list of conditions that could render a child eligible for services under this part. The language relating to other health impairments is also modified to clarify that limited strength, vitality, or alertness includes a child's heightened alertness to environmental stimuli that results in limited alertness with respect to the educational environment.

There have been dramatic changes in the procedures for identifying students with learning disabilities. Many of the changes are covered in the Response to Intervention section of this chapter. It is important to point out, however, that learning disabilities covers the largest category of students receiving special education services.

6

What Is an IEP, and
What Is the Principal's Role?

The individualized education program (IEP) is the most important document that
exists for a student with a disability. For all practical purposes, view the IEP
as a contract between the district and the parents or guardians of the student.
The IEP formalizes a student's education, listing the education and intervention
services provided for the student. The courts have held in the past that failure
to properly develop and implement an IEP can invalidate a program.

PURPOSES OF THE IEP

The IEP serves many purposes: instructional, communication, management,
accountability, monitoring, compliance, and evaluation.

Instructional

As an *instructional* tool, the IEP delineates the services provided to the student. It
should include: general identification information about the student, present level of
functioning with a description of the current placement, recommendations from the
committee that evaluated the student, instructional goals (including a statement of
how those will be evaluated), and a statement of classroom modifications. It should
also include other services the student requires. As an instructional tool, a student
should be able to transfer between districts with the new teacher(s) picking up the IEP
and knowing exactly what is required for this student.

Communication

As a *communication* tool, the IEP serves several functions. The first function it serves
is that of keeping all the individuals who are a part of the student's life (most notably
the parents) informed about the education the student is receiving. The development

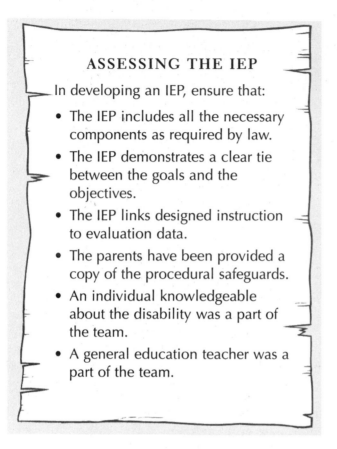

ASSESSING THE IEP

In developing an IEP, ensure that:

• The IEP includes all the necessary components as required by law.

• The IEP demonstrates a clear tie between the goals and the objectives.

• The IEP links designed instruction to evaluation data.

• The parents have been provided a copy of the procedural safeguards.

• An individual knowledgeable about the disability was a part of the team.

• A general education teacher was a part of the team.

of the IEP should be a truly collaborative effort.

Management

The IEP serves a very important function as a *management* device. In addition to detailing the supports, services, and accommodations required in the general or special education classroom, it should indicate whether or not a child needs special counseling, special transportation, an aide, or other related services. A principal should be able to read an IEP and easily understand which professionals are providing services to this child and for how long each day; because of this, the IEP serves a very important role in staff allocation and planning.

Accountability

Another important function of the IEP is that of *accountability*. The IEP serves as a contract between the district and the parents; by completing the IEP, the district has contracted to commit resources to the student. For example, if it is stated in the IEP that a student is to receive 2 hours of instruction five times a week from a special education teacher, the student must receive 2 hours a day of instruction from a special education teacher, not an aide or other professional or paraprofessional. If the student is only receiving 1 hour of instruction a day, this does not satisfy the IEP. If, however either one of these adaptations better suits the child's needs, then the IEP should be changed to reflect those needs.

Some have the impression that when we talk about the IEP as an instrument of accountability that means that the district will be held liable for the student not meeting the goals of the IEP. This is not what the law implies, and should not be inferred. An appropriate IEP is one in which the district has made a good-faith effort to implement the IEP, kept track of their efforts, and when problems occurred, worked to change. If, however, the district does not make good-faith efforts to implement the IEP or respond to problems or parental concerns, then the IEP is inappropriate.

Monitoring, Compliance, and Evaluation

The next major function of the IEP is its use as a *monitoring* or *compliance* device. Principals need to learn the components of an IEP and ensure all services are appropriately delineated in the document. When outside agencies or compliance officers from state boards of education review programs for students with disabilities, the first place they look is the IEP of each student. The IEP is the "point of contact" where monitoring occurs to see if students with disabilities are being provided a free appropriate public education.

The last main function of the IEP is *evaluation*. Although a district will most likely not be held accountable for not meeting the IEP goals as long as they have made a good-faith effort, IEP goals help determine whether a student is making progress. This is an important point to keep in mind when writing the IEP, and when reviewing it. Additionally, write the goals and objectives behaviorally to help clarify whether or not an individual has achieved a goal.

THE IEP TEAM

The Individuals with Disabilities Education Act (IDEA) dictates that the "public agency" providing educational services must ensure that the IEP team includes: the parents of the child with a disability; at least one general education teacher of the child (if the child is, or may be, participating in the general education environment); at least one special education teacher of the child, or one special education provider; and a representative of the public agency who is qualified to provide, or supervise the provision of, specially designed instruction to meet the unique needs of children with disabilities, is knowledgeable about the general education curriculum, and is knowledgeable about the availability of resources of the public agency. This "representative of the public agency" is also referred to as the local education agency (LEA). The LEA very well might be the principal or assistant principal of the school, or it could be the district's special education administrator.

Other IEP team members include an individual who can interpret the instructional implications of evaluation results; other individuals who have knowledge or special expertise regarding the child, including related services personnel as appropriate (at the discretion of the parent or the agency); and when appropriate, the child with a disability (IDEA, 1990; also see Chapter 3). The team's purpose is to address the educational needs of the student; every individual involved in this effort, no matter how limited his or her role, thereby gets the "big picture."

The first IEP meeting must be held within 30 calendar days of issuance of the initial evaluation report. The child must start receiving services in the IEP no later than 10 school days after the parent has approved the IEP. If you cannot write the IEP within that period because of extenuating circumstances, you need to document the reasons for this, and ensure it is written as soon as possible.

The 1997 IDEA amendments require that general education teachers participate in IEP development. An increasing number of students with disabilities are being educated in the general education classroom environment; including the general education teacher ensures that everyone who works with a particular student gets information that will assist them on a day-to-day basis. It also provides an opportunity for general education teachers to understand the many facets of special education.

WHAT PARENTS NEED TO KNOW

After parents have attended an IEP meeting they should have a clear understanding of the following:

- Why their child needs special education.
- Who will be providing the services.
- Where the services are to be provided.
- The duration of the services.
- The schedule for evaluation.
- How much time their child will spend in the general education classroom.
- What other services are going to be provided to their child, such as transportation or counseling.

Parental Involvement

As mentioned above, the IEP itself provides a means of specifically communicating to parents the educational interventions and services provided to their children. Having an opportunity to sit down and discuss what their child should learn and the methods used, and the amount of time provided to meet those needs, is not afforded most parents of children without disabilities. This does not mean that the parents can sit down and dictate what, where, and by whom. However, staff members should listen to parental concerns and make an effort to address them as much as possible.

Student Participation

Students 16 years of age or older must be involved in the development of their IEP. Why 16? This is the age that the regulations state we must start to develop a transition plan as a part of the student's IEP:

the public agency must invite a child with a disability to attend the child's IEP meeting if a purpose of the meeting will be the consideration of the postsecondary goals for the child and the transition services needed to assist the child in reaching those goals under §300.320(b) (IDEA 2004, Section 300.321(b)1)).

A transition plan is the enumeration of the steps and goals for postsecondary life, and the specific methods to assist the student in achieving those goals (see "Transition Statement," below); the student must be invited to participate in the development of this plan.

PREPARING FOR THE IEP MEETING

Preparing for the IEP meeting requires a lot of background work. By reviewing the documents and asking questions, one can walk into an IEP meeting not only with an understanding of what this particular IEP should include, but also prepared to respond to any questions that arise during the process. Increasingly it is the principal who schedules, assists in development, and signs the IEP as representative of the school district. Even if the director of special education holds the meetings, principals still need to be informed; knowing the needs of students with disabilities at your school enables you to ensure that your school's resources are adequate for your student population. Additionally, many principals are called upon to step in at the last minute to chair and conduct such meetings; not being prepared does not effectively serve the district's interests. If you are the least bit unsure about certain educational interventions, and believe the recommended services might be excessive (or too little), seek clarification from your supervisor. For example, one principal acting as district representative signed 32 IEPs stating that the students would have access to computers 100% of the time. Because of a due process hearing (see Chapters 3 and 9), the district had to purchase 32 computers. So be sure the district can (and will) provide these things before you agree to them and sign on the line.

✓ *Review the referral and evaluation(s)*

Pay close attention to the referral for testing and any academic problems that may have been presented in the past. Additionally, determine the student's strengths and weaknesses from the evaluation report. The student's strengths should form the basis for IEP development.

✓ *Talk to the team*

Talk to individuals who were a part of the multidisciplinary team about their impressions of the education this student should receive. Also, talk to them about any part(s) of the team report that either you do not understand or with which you need clarification.

✓ *Review previous IEPs*

Specifically, look at the goals listed on the student's previous IEPs and compare them with the results of the evaluation reports. If possible, talk with the teachers who implemented previous IEPs, and ask them for suggestions about what worked, what did not work, and what they might do differently.

✓ *Talk to special education and general education teachers*

The *special education teacher* most likely has responsibility for implementing the student's new IEP, and so will have valuable recommendations for educating this student. (We say "most likely" instead of "will" because where the student will be educated and who will be providing those services are team decisions at the IEP meeting.)

Current and past teachers will have insights about what has worked with this student, and where there have been problems. This information will help establish the educational programming the student should receive.

You may need to evaluate the caseload or numbers of students for different teachers or related service personnel. State departments of education have strict guidelines about class sizes in special education classrooms. While it might not be your responsibility to monitor this number, you may need to bring it to others' attention if the numbers are too high.

Who is the *general education teacher* most likely to be involved in the education of this student? Sometimes only the current classroom teacher is involved, and the student receives resource assistance for a small part of the day. In other cases, however, the student is in secondary school and because of the severity of the disability needs to be educated in a separate facility. In this case, the general education teacher most likely to interact with the student if he or she were to attend your school should be included in IEP development.

✓ *Set a time and place for the meeting*

The time should be convenient to the parents; do your best to get them involved, even if it takes several telephone calls or notices sent home, or even if you need to make alternate arrangements such as allowing them to participate via conference call.

Congress has stipulated that the IEP is a form of communication between the school and the parents; you have to both make an effort to get them to the meeting, and for your own protection document your efforts to do so.

The time for the meeting should also be convenient for the special education teacher who is most likely to be implementing the plan. Although you have already sought the teacher's input, you need this teacher to help make decisions regarding what can and cannot be done in the classroom and with limited time. You might realize through this process that a different special education teacher is more appropriate for a particular student, or that the identified special education teacher is currently overwhelmed by responsibilities or student caseload.

✓ *Draft an IEP*

Developing draft sections of some components of the IEP is a timesaving practice. Some districts assign an individual to develop a draft before the meeting; this should be someone who is familiar with the student, has knowledge about the student's disability, and who is experienced at writing IEPs. If you follow this procedure, remember that the emphasis should be on the word "draft." Advise those attending that this is only a draft. You can make additions, delete or reword passages, or rewrite the whole document. Make sure all participants in the meeting understand that this can be done.

✓ *Observe the student*

Note the student's academic and social behavior, and how he or she handles frustration. Observe interaction with other students, where the student goes for assistance, and how well organized he or she appears. Also provide opportunities for observations by an individual who is knowledgeable about the disability, or who might be the one responsible for implementing the IEP. Yes, they will get to know the student after the IEP meeting, but this will help him or her in providing guidance during the development of the IEP.

Finally, make sure the parents are aware they can invite someone they view as knowledgeable about their child's disability to provide assistance in the development of the IEP (this is new to the regulations).

While preparing for an IEP meeting might seem involved, each individual step, as a part of the information gathering process, does not have to be long, and these points do not have to be accomplished in any particular sequence. Many principals meet with the teachers as they are walking down the hall or standing in the lunchroom, for example. The important thing is to keep these questions in mind in order to be sufficiently prepared for the meeting.

Logistics

The actual location of the meeting is not an immaterial element. Some parents want to keep the proceedings as confidential as possible, while for others that is not a problem. Avoid holding the meeting in an office in which there might be questions of privacy. Make sure participants have comfortable chairs, water, and a break if the meeting takes over an hour. The room should be as free from distractions as possible. You may need special equipment to enable essential individuals to participate by telephone. Because the development of the IEP is a team process, you may want to use a chalkboard or easel to jot down ideas. Finally, make it easier for teachers to participate by arranging coverage for their classes.

THE IEP MEETING

Developing an IEP is a collaborative process, and all ideas need to be addressed. Participants should not feel rushed; avoid "educationese" and acronyms, but if you need to use these terms, explain them without being condescending. All ideas need to be considered impartially, and someone should keep notes of the meeting.

✓ Make sure the parents understand the definition and purpose(s) of the IEP, and the purpose of the meeting itself. This individualized education program exists for their child only; a student with a similar disability very well might have different goals and objectives. The purpose of the meeting is to plan the special education program for their child. Invite parental input on the plan.

✓ Make sure that the parents understand that the plan is continually evaluated over the course of the year, and if they find that things are not working as planned, another IEP meeting could occur.

✓ Introduce everyone at the meeting, explaining the different roles these individuals will play in the education of the child. Explain that your own role is to help guide the group through the development of the IEP. If they have questions at any time they should ask, and make sure you clarify everything.

✓ If you are presenting a draft IEP, ensure that the parents understand that it is a draft and that they can make comments or offer additions or deletions.

Essential Questions

If any answer is "yes," these issues must be addressed in the IEP.

✓ Is the student blind or visually impaired?

✓ Is the student deaf or hearing impaired?

✓ Does the student exhibit behaviors that impede his or her learning or that of others?

✓ Does the student have limited English proficiency?

✓ Does the student require assistive technology devices and services?

✓ Does the student need transition services?

✓ Will the student be 16 years of age or older within the duration of this IEP?

✓ Is the student within 3 years of graduation?

✓ Will this student potentially qualify for extended school year services (ESY)?

✓ Does this student need adaptive physical education?

✓ Are there any related services that this student needs?

✓ Will this student participate in statewide assessments?

IEP Elements

The meeting needs to establish essential elements of the student's IEP (see "IEP Components" below), including present level of performance, academic areas in which the student needs assistance, social/emotional areas in which the student needs assistance, amount of time the student will spend in the general education classroom (or other discussion of the student's interaction with nondisabled peers), and when the IEP will be evaluated. Every IEP must be evaluated at least annually. However, parents also need to be aware of how their child is doing in relation to the IEP goals as frequently as parents of nondisabled children are notified. This means that if other students in the school get a report card every 9 weeks, then the students with disabilities should get an IEP progress report every 9 weeks as well.

Managing the Meeting

Some parents may not want to spend much time at an IEP meeting; they will come to the meeting and say, "Where do I sign?" They trust the district, or perhaps they have been through the process so many times, and they are tired of the same meetings with the same people. Whatever the reason, they should still be encouraged to stay long enough to give the school staff the assurance that they understand what is going on.

On the other hand, there are parents who know special education law better than a school district attorney, or parents who bring an advocate with them to help them make sense of the meeting. This can be scary for some principals or IEP meeting leaders. It is important to remember that the parent may have brought this individual in an effort to better understand what is being recommended and decided; they just want the best for their child.

The purpose of the IEP meeting is to work together to meet the student's special needs.

While it may very well take more than one session to complete a student's IEP, you still need to ensure that each meeting is run as efficiently as possible. Keep the participants focused on the goals and objectives included in the IEP, review what has worked during the past year, and discuss changes for next year's IEP.

Record keeping is a very important part of the process. This will provide you with accurate coverage of what transpired, and may come in handy in the event there is some disagreement about what was actually agreed to at the meeting.

AFTER THE IEP MEETING

Getting the IEP signed by all the parties that will be working with the student is an important part of the process. However, the most important part of the process is to make sure that the IEP is meeting the student's needs.

✓ Provide the parents with a signed copy of the IEP.

✓ Provide copies of the IEP to the teacher(s) who will be working to implement the IEP.

✓ Touch base with teachers on a monthly basis to get feedback on all your students' IEPs. This helps you in monitoring whether an individual student's needs are being met.

✓ At least once every 9 weeks, meet with the special education teachers and determine if the students with IEPs are making progress toward the goals on the IEP.

✓ Send notices to parents about student progress toward IEP goals as frequently as other students are getting report cards (see "IEP Components" discussion of progress reports, below).

✓ If a student is not meeting the goals of the IEP, or it appears the IEP needs to be changed, arrange another IEP meeting as soon as possible.

Be sure to document all these steps with at least a brief summary of when the item was conducted or completed, notes from conversations with teachers, dates of meetings, and so on. Such meetings are merely a means of monitoring student progress, and help you assess whether the student needs additional time and services or, alternatively, reduced time and services.

IEPS FROM OTHER DISTRICTS

If a student arrives at your school with an IEP from another school district, you are obligated to implement services comparable to those described in the existing IEP until your school district adopts the previous IEP or implements a new IEP. This can make planning difficult; you might have planned staffing and resources for the current year and had everything well organized, and one or two students with identified disabilities could throw off the whole plan. You may rewrite the IEP to meet the specifics of your building and your personnel; this new transitional IEP should be in place within a week after you receive the old IEP. You cannot change the education and interventions provided to the student just because he or she is starting in your school. For instance, you cannot take a child receiving services for a learning disability in a self-contained day school in the previous district, and switch him into the general education classroom with only intermittent supports.

As the IEP the student brought is valid until a new IEP is developed, your next step is to convene an IEP meeting for the new student. You should use the information in the existing IEP to assist in developing a new IEP.

WORKING WITH PARENTS

As stated previously, you have to make concerted attempts to involve parents in the IEP process. If you must hold an IEP meeting without the parents, you need to document the steps you took to involve the parents, including a record of the phone calls made or attempted, when they occurred, and by whom, and any results of those calls; and copies of any letters or notes sent to the parents regarding the meeting with a description of responses. Also, attempt to obtain a copy of the parents' email address and use that in addition to the mailing of the letters. If you cannot reach the parents via telephone, or they do not respond to letters or notes sent home, keep a record of visits to the home or place of employment, to include descriptions of time, date, who, and the results of any conversations about the upcoming meeting.

Additionally, make every effort to ensure that the parents understand what is going on during the meeting. You may need to provide an interpreter for parents who use sign language, or for parents whose preferred language is not English. Take time during the meeting to make sure the parents understand the process and the terminology, and that they understand in what environment their child will be educated and for what purpose.

What if the Parents Do Not Sign the IEP?

There are many reasons why a parent might not sign an IEP. They might not believe in special education, they might not want their child pulled out of the general education class, or they might want more educational interventions than the district has proposed. This does not happen very often, but if it does, there are some solutions.

If a parent does not sign the IEP, the district has several choices. An important point to remember is the parents may have a very good reason why they are not signing the IEP. The first thing to do is determine why the parents have refused to sign the IEP. The reasons for their actions will steer your next steps, and will help your district make decisions about the next steps.

If the parents refuse to sign the IEP because they feel their child is nondisabled, there are several important steps. First, explain to the parents that a multidisciplinary team meeting determined their child did have a disability. Second, explain that the purpose of the IEP meeting is to develop the education plan based on the decisions made at the prior meeting. If the parents are unhappy with the results of the multidisciplinary meeting, they have the right to an independent evaluation that may assist in providing information about school-related problems their child might be having (see Chapter 5).

If the parents refuse to sign the IEP because they do not want their child sent to a "special" class, explain the reasoning behind the use of a self-contained setting. You also need to analyze the structure of how you are providing services to students with disabilities. Is a separate location necessary, or can the same services be provided to the student (and others who might be having problems) in the general education classroom? (See Chapter 7 for more information about issues relating to inclusion.)

If the parents do not sign the IEP because they feel you are not providing appropriate interventions, you need to explain the rationale behind your recommendations. If you are recommending that the student spend only part of the day with a special education teacher, your basis is that the purpose of the law is for students to receive education with their nondisabled peers to the maximum extent possible. If the student is receiving his or her education in a self-contained classroom and the parents request a more restrictive setting, describe the rationale behind selecting the regular school as the location. Explain to the parents that if there are problems in this placement, a change to a more restrictive setting can occur during the school year. Again, analyze the educational interventions and services that you are recommending for this student. Are they appropriate?

If you cannot reach agreement, refer to the previous agreed-upon IEP, assuming there is one. If there is no IEP, is there any agreement at all? For instance, there might be agreement that the student needs speech therapy on a regular basis but no agreement on whether assistance for reading is necessary. If this is the case, then write an IEP for the areas of agreement, listing areas of disagreement. Then work to implement that written, approved IEP.

If there are major areas of disagreement, remind the parents of their right for mediation, complaint, or a due process hearing. The district has the same rights (see Chapters 3 and 9). If there is an ongoing due process hearing, the old IEP or the IEP to which they agreed *is the IEP that is in place pending the hearing officer's decision.* For instance, if the student is placed in the general education classroom and a subsequent disagreement arises over placement, the child remains in the general education classroom until the final decision, unless the parties come to some other agreement. This would also hold true if the student were in a special school before the discussions of the new IEP; he or she would stay there until the final decision by the hearing officer. This is true even if the decision takes months to reach.

IEP COMPONENTS

Federal regulations are very specific about what needs to be included as a part of a student's IEP. Your state may have additional rules or regulations as a part of the process.

Present Level of Performance

What are the student's current levels of academic achievement and functional performance? What can we learn from the latest evaluations? What can the parents add to descriptions of performance? Teachers? Can the child learn and progress in the general education curriculum?

The *present level of performance* is often the first item of business addressed in an IEP meeting. If the participants can agree to the student's current level of functioning, then it's much easier to move on to discussing measurable academic and functional annual goals and short-term objectives. The present level of performance statement should describe the academic and/or behavioral levels of the student, relating this to the general education curriculum, and establishing the reasons why this student needs an IEP. The statement might include the academic areas in which the student has problems, his or her strengths, areas where the student needs assistance in mobility or daily living, and a description of prevocational or vocational skills. Including test scores is appropriate, but they are not the sole measure; you use test scores (such as a grade equivalent score on the Woodcock Reading Mastery Test-Revised/Normative Update of 4.5), you also need to clarify the student's strengths and weaknesses and explain the grade equivalent. The use of curriculum-based measures is encouraged; however, you need to include descriptors of where these measures are taken, and what the scores really mean. For example, stating the student is on "Level Eight" may mean nothing to another individual implementing the IEP.

It is all right to use a label such as a *learning disability* or *mental retardation*. However, it is not all right to use these in place of the descriptors listed above.

When writing the present level of performance section, keep in mind that students with disabilities are often highly transient. Other schools' staff should be able to look at the IEP description of present level of performance and be able to make two statements:

I really know this student's level of performance, and knowing this will make implementing this student's IEP easier in my district, and

The individual who led the meeting in the development of the IEP really knows his or her information.

If the forms your district uses are too small to include the all the information as listed above, add additional sheets. You really will benefit the child by including as much as you can.

Information for the present level of performance should come directly from the report issued by the multidisciplinary team, supplemented by information resulting from your pre-IEP meeting discussions with members of the multidisciplinary team and previous classroom teachers, and from observations of the student in the classroom. If you need assistance in determining present levels of performance from the report written by the multidisciplinary team, make sure you ask questions prior to the IEP meeting. For instance, if you are going to be writing that the "DTLA-4 states there is a discrepancy in his reading," and someone asks you what the "DTLA-4" is and what it measures, make sure you can answer. Try to avoid using terms that noneducators would find confusing.

Measurable Academic and Functional Annual Goals

What does the IEP team want the student to learn this year? What goals are needed for the child to be involved in and progress in the general education curriculum? Do the goals reflect all the student's disability-related needs?

The IEP should have an *annual goal* for each area in which the student might need assistance, such as reading, math, or writing, not short-term objectives or benchmarks, which should be covered separately (see below).

Typically, the annual goals are the second item of business as a part of the IEP meeting. They become the broad areas of agreement that the team needs to address. This assumes there is agreement (see "What if the Parents Do Not Sign the IEP?," above). Work to get agreement on the broad annual goals before moving on to other areas. The annual goals are developed not only from the multidisciplinary team report, but also from interviews with previous teachers, current teachers, observations, and the parent's statement of needs.

Short-Term Objectives

What are the benchmarks for measuring short-term progress toward IEP goals?

Short-term objectives is the historical term for the steps under the annual goals. The 1997 IDEA amendments changed the term to include benchmarks, to emphasize that the short-term objectives or benchmarks are steps to the student achieving an annual goal. After you have agreement on the present level of performance and the annual goals, develop the *short-term objectives or benchmarks* to meet those annual goals. Additionally, developing short-term objectives or benchmarks clarifies the needed services the student should be receiving.

The 2004 IDEA amendments removed short-term instructional objectives as a requirement for students who take regular state assessments. Short-term instructional objectives are only mandatory for students who take alternative assessments aligned to alternate achievement standards.

The short-term objectives or benchmarks come directly from the present level of performance and the services the student needs to meet the IEP goals. For example, if a 12-year-old student has an IQ of 49 and is reading at the kindergarten level with numerous errors and little comprehension, an expected service might be a highly structured reading program 5 days a week. The annual goal would be to improve the student's reading to the first-grade level with 0-3 errors per 20 words. This annual goal is used to develop the short-term objectives for the end of November, the end of February, and the end of May. The short-term objectives build upon themselves, and are a monitoring device.

An important part of the short-term objectives is that they include evaluation procedures, criteria, and a schedule. Following the example from above, if a student is expected to meet a goal by the end of November, then there also needs to be progress monitoring addressing the goal.

Short-term objectives need to include:

1. Statement tied to the annual goals of the instruction.
2. How the goal will be provided.
3. A description of the criteria for achieving the goal.
4. When an evaluation will occur.

Short-term objectives or benchmarks allow the teacher and the parents to see if the student is making progress. They are the part of the IEP that is adapted during the course of the year if the benchmarks either are not attained or are attained too quickly. The reason for monthly meetings is to be able to make changes to the IEP when necessary instead of waiting until the end of the year and then talking about which benchmarks were inappropriate.

**THINGS
TO CONSIDER**

- Does the child need special education for only some part of the day? Most of the day? All of the day?
- What type of special education service does the child need? What type of support does the child need?

Specific Special Education Program to Be Provided

What specialized instruction, methods, and strategies will school personnel use to help the child progress towards the IEP goals, to be involved and make progress in the general education curriculum, and to participate in extracurricular and nonacademic activities? Where will the services be provided?

This part of the student's IEP assists in the administrative task of keeping track of the amount of contact hours the teachers have with students, and the number of students for which they are responsible. Every IEP should list the specific services provided to the student, including special education services; related services necessary for the student to benefit from special education; and supports, accommodations or modifications in the general education classroom. Additionally, the IEP should include the location of the services the student is expected to receive, the number of hours a week, and when the services will end. This information must be clear to all the attendees of the meeting and to any other individual who might read the IEP (for example, if the student were to move to another school district).

Supplementary Aids, Services, and Modifications

Are changes to the program or extra supports needed to help the child succeed in general education classes? What extra help will be provided to the child and to the child's teacher so the child can advance toward annual goals, be involved and progress in the general curriculum, be educated with nondisabled peers, and participate in state and districtwide assessments?

The regulations state that IEP teams should make "a determination as to whether any modifications to the special education and related services are needed to enable the child to meet the annual goals set out in the IEP of the child and to participate, as appropriate, in the general curriculum" (34 C.F.R. § 300.305(a)(2)(iv).

In 1997, Congress amended the law to state that all students with disabilities will participate in district-wide and state assessments. However, some students need modifications in order to participate, and these necessary modifications must be incorporated into the IEP. Examples include reading a math assessment to students who are visually impaired or blind, or extended time allowed for some students with learning disabilities. Again, the rationale behind this is to encourage teachers to think of the students with disabilities as a part of the general education classroom, and to encourage teachers to provide access to these students to the general curriculum.

Some students, even with modifications, would not receive an accurate assessment. In this case, the IEP needs to delineate why the assessment is not appropriate and should describe alternative forms of assessments to be used instead of the districtwide or state assessments (such as normative individual assessments; see below, "Legislative Guidelines for Alternate Assessments").

Type, Amount, and Frequency of Related Services

What types of related services, such as transportation or physical, occupational, or speech therapy, does the child need? How often will it be provided? How much time for each session?

Related services are the educational services and interventions necessary for the student to benefit from education. Recently, the Supreme Court reaffirmed the necessity of related services, and defined related services as those performed in the school, but not those performed by a physician (*Cedar Rapids Community School District v Garrett*, 1999).

The IDEA 2004 requirements reinforce the emphasis on progress in the general curriculum, as well as maximizing the extent to which children with disabilities are educated with nondisabled children, describing related services as those that are

> required to assist a child with a disability to benefit from special education, and includes speech-language pathology and audiology services, interpreting services, psychological services, physical and occupational therapy, recreation, including therapeutic recreation, counseling services, including rehabilitation counseling, orientation and mobility services, and medical services for diagnostic or evaluation purposes. Related services also includes school health services, school nurse services designed to enable a child with a disability to receive a free appropriate public education as described in the IEP of the child, social work services in schools, and parent counseling and training. (34 C.F.R. § 300.34)

The Extent That the Student Will Participate With Students Without Disabilities

If the child cannot be in general education classes for the full school day, during which parts of the school day will the child be with children without disabilities?

All student IEPs must include a statement about how much time they will participate with nondisabled students (including general education classrooms, extracurricular activities, social outings, and before/after school activities). The presumption of the law is that students with disabilities will be educated to the "maximum extent appropriate to the needs of that child" (34 C.F.R. 300.117) with nondisabled students (see also Chapter 7).

The general education classroom is the presumed placement for students with disabilities, unless it can be shown they would benefit from being placed in a different setting.

The law goes on to state that:

> special classes, separate schooling or other removal of children with disabilities from the regular educational environment occurs only if the nature or severity of the disability is such that education in regular classes with the use of supplementary aids and services cannot be achieved satisfactorily. (20 U.S.C. 612(a)(5)(A))

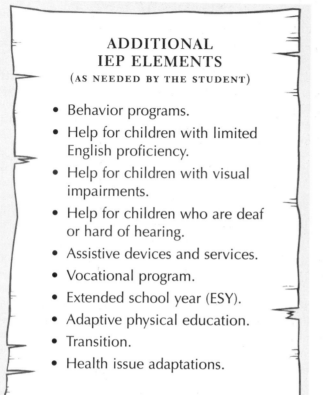

**ADDITIONAL
IEP ELEMENTS**

(AS NEEDED BY THE STUDENT)

- Behavior programs.
- Help for children with limited English proficiency.
- Help for children with visual impairments.
- Help for children who are deaf or hard of hearing.
- Assistive devices and services.
- Vocational program.
- Extended school year (ESY).
- Adaptive physical education.
- Transition.
- Health issue adaptations.

Location of Services

What environment is recommended for the child? Can the services on the IEP be delivered in that school? Is there any reason the IEP cannot be implemented in the school the child would attend if not disabled? Is the placement as close to the home as possible?

School districts must offer a continuum of alternative placements to meet the needs of children with disabilities, including "instruction in regular classes, in special classes of schools, home instruction with the child not to be removed from education in age-appropriate regular education solely because of needed modifications in the general curriculum" (34 C.F.R. 300.116 (IDEA 2004)). In addition, section 300.116 now provides for the placement decision to made "in conformity with the [least restrictive environment] provisions." Placement should be as close as possible to the child's home, with the child being educated in the school he or she would attend if nondisabled; the law states specifically that "unless the IEP of a child with a disability requires some other arrangement, the child in the school that he or she would attend if nondisabled, unless the parent agrees otherwise" (34 C.F.R. § 300.116(C)).

Dates Services Begin and End

When will the services begin? Immediately? Will all the services continue through the school year?

The student cannot begin to receive special education services before the signing of an IEP.

The IEP must include the duration of the services to be provided. Many IEPs specify the duration of the services for the inclusive dates of the school year; if an IEP is written for a calendar year, the school district would be required to provide extended school year services to a student who might not need such services. If you do not expect a student to receive extended school year (ESY) services, the IEP should specify that services are for the academic year only. However, you should always consider whether the student needs ESY services, and note this consideration and decision within the IEP.

How to Determine if the Child Is Making Progress

Are the annual goals and short-term objectives really measurable? How will the IEP team measure the progress the child makes? How and when will the parents be informed of the child's progress?

The IEP must include measurable annual goals "to enable the child to be involved in and progress in the general curriculum" (34 C.F.R. Section 300.320(a)(2)(i)(A)). The IEP must incorporate a method of notifying parents of the student's progress. Parents can request an IEP meeting at any time in the process. As noted earlier, the IEP should be evaluated at least once a year. The purpose of this review is to revise the IEP based on the child's progress (or lack of progress), his or her annual goals, any evaluations or reevaluations, and teacher and parent concerns.

It is also expected that parents be informed of the progress their child is making in school relating to the IEP goals and objectives. This can include progress notes on a student's particular goals, indicating that the goal is met, that it is being addressed, that the student is at a particular level of competency, or that the goal has not been attempted. Not every IEP goal would necessarily be addressed during each report period

Providing statements about goals further reinforces the IEP as a method of *accountability*. If the IEP states certain goals will be addressed by a certain date, and progress is not forthcoming, this assists you in making decisions about whether the IEP should be revised. In addition to monthly meetings with special education teachers about student IEP goals, principals should review notices sent home about IEP goals and the progress made toward them.

Transition Statement

Transition services legally means a coordinated set of activities for a student with a disability that is "focused on improving the academic and functional achievement of the child with a disability to facilitate the child's movement from school to post school activities, including postsecondary education, vocational education, integrated employment (including supported employment), continuing and adult education, adult services, independent living, or community participation" (IDEA, 20 U.S.C. 1401(34)).

If the student turns 16 during the year of the IEP, the IEP must include a *transition statement* describing the steps necessary to prepare this student for post-high school life. Three main factors brought about the requirement for transition services: the high unemployment rate for individuals with disabilities, the realization that students with disabilities were leaving a free appropriate public education and entering a system where their rights and supports were very different, and the realization that students educated in special education were not achieving desired outcomes. These historical changes and changes in public policy over time paved the way for these regulations, established by the Individuals with Disabilities Education Act in 1990.

There are many different types of appropriate transition programs, including vocational education, supported employment, meeting with college counselors, and meeting with group home staff. Each program needs to be individualized, reviewed annually, and revised if necessary depending on the needs of the student.

Because of the changes in the law,

➡ Parents and school personnel are thinking about what is going to happen to the student after high school before the student gets to the graduation year.

➡ Schools are having to think about who will be responsible for working with the student after they leave school.

➡ Schools are having to communicate and collaborate with external agencies in planning for the student.

➡ Schools are now starting to be held accountable for getting the students ready for postschool life.

➡ Planning for transition for students with disabilities is starting at a younger age (elementary) and this is benefiting all involved.

LEGISLATIVE GUIDELINES FOR ALTERNATE ASSESSMENTS

The law requires that children with disabilities be included in state and districtwide assessment programs, "with appropriate accommodations and alternate assessments, if necessary, and as indicated in their respective IEPs" (§300.160). The state (or district, in the case of a district-wide assessment) must develop guidelines for providing appropriate accommodations and for conducting alternate assessments. Alternate assessments must be "aligned with the State's challenging academic content standards and challenging student academic achievement standards; and . . . measure the achievement of children with disabilities against those standards" (18 § 300.160).

7 What Does a Principal Need to Know About Inclusion?

Few topics regarding the education of students with disabilities have generated as much controversy as the debate surrounding inclusion. It is important for principals to know the history of inclusion, the different approaches and methods for providing services to students with disabilities, and what the law says (and does not say) about inclusion. . . . Inclusion applies to students eligible for special education, as well as those labeled as gifted and talented, and those who are considered at risk. For the principal, inclusion requires a focus on a variety of instructional variables impacting the education of all students.

Inclusion can be described as the meaningful participation of students with special needs in general education classrooms and programs. But what is "meaningful participation"? Admittedly, the practice of inclusion varies from one school district to another, and even among schools within the same district. Some schools may have a policy of full inclusion, regardless of the severity of disability, while others interpret inclusion as occasions where students with disabilities spend some time in the general education classroom.

How do current inclusive practices relate to federal law and the concepts of alternative placements and education in the least restrictive environment? How did our current practices of inclusion evolve?

A BRIEF HISTORY OF INCLUSION

Some principals feel that implementing inclusion was thrust upon general educators without warning, historical rationale, or preparation. Only the last one of those three is partially right. The principle of inclusion has a long history, though it was sometimes expressed in other words or ideas. There are different terms associated with inclusion, each signifying a different historical period. Those terms are *mainstreaming*, the *Regular Education Initiative, inclusion,* and *full inclusion.* They are not synonyms, although they often are used interchangeably. Each signifies not only a period in the development of inclusion but also a philosophical stance regarding the environment in which students with disabilities should be educated.

Mainstreaming

Mainstreaming was a term used in describing the education of students with disabilities in the 1970s and early 1980s. It refers generally to working to include students with disabilities in general education, although a student with a disability would spend most, if not all, of the school day in the special education class. When the student demonstrated he or she was well behaved and could handle the academic curriculum, the student would be mainstreamed into the general education classroom for part of a day. Students were considered mainstreamed if they spent *any* part of the day with the general education class. Most students with a disability spent most of the day with the special education teacher, and went to the mainstream class for nonacademic activities such as lunch or recess. (Mainstreaming parallels a period in adult services when there existed a movement to involve institutionalized individuals in the community, often referred to as deinstitutionalization.)

Only students with mild disabilities such as learning disabilities or mild mental retardation participated in mainstreaming. Students with more severe disabilities and those with behavior problems had no real opportunity to participate with their peers. Even those students with mild disabilities often had little, if any, real opportunity for meaningful participation and the development of long-term relationships. This was further exacerbated by the fact that many general education teachers felt students with disabilities were the responsibility of special education teachers and that these students were just added on in activities that really did not count.

The goal of mainstreaming was integration for some part of the day for the purposes of instructional and social integration.

Mainstreaming worked better in some locations than it did in others. It was supposed to vary with the needs of the individual student, with those who needed more support receiving appropriate attention while others who did not need additional support being educated in the general education classroom. Problems with mainstreaming included a lack of individualization (e.g., all students with mental retardation went to special education), and the idea that students with mild disabilities had to "earn" their place in the general education setting.

The Regular Education Initiative

Though mainstreaming worked for some students, it did not work for many—especially students with severe disabilities. In addition, the education community continued to consider students with disabilities to be the responsibility of special education teachers and staff. In 1986, Assistant Secretary of Education Madeleine Will launched the Regular Education Initiative (REI), proposing that general education teachers and staff assume more responsibility for educating students with disabilities.

REI shifted the responsibility of educating students with disabilities from special education to general education.

This might seem like a subtle shift, but it represents a major philosophical shift in providing services to meet the needs of students with disabilities. Previously, when a student was found eligible for special education, the student became the responsibility of special education. Now, there was the expectation the student would receive special education services but would still participate in the general education classroom. In addition, the general education teacher assumed responsibility for at least part of the student's education. REI helped change the debate about the provision of services, and it laid the foundation for inclusion.

Inclusion

Although the debate shifted under REI, some students with severe disabilities still did not get the chance to participate in general education. *Inclusion*, the term currently used, promotes the education of all students in the general education classroom environment. Under *full inclusion*, services to at-risk students, students with disabilities, or students with exceptionalities are not provided in other locations; those services come to them in the general education classroom.

The presumption under inclusion is that the student with a disability will participate fully, both academically and socially, in the general education classroom. This requires that the necessary supports for students with special needs are available in this environment. Additionally, the general education teacher is expected to vary her teaching methods and classroom routines, procedures and processes so all students will benefit from instruction. The student with a disability remains in the general education classroom unless all available methods have been exhausted in an effort to meet his or her needs. If, after every available method is tried in the general education classroom and the student's needs are not met, then he or she may be pulled out for additional services. This pullout is temporary, with the goal of returning the student to the general education classroom as soon as possible.

WHAT DO FEDERAL REGULATIONS SAY ABOUT INCLUSION?

The federal government has indicated support for the principles of inclusion in IDEA 2004. The presumption of the law is that:

> to the maximum extent appropriate, children with disabilities, including children in public or private institutions or other care facilities, are educated with children who are nondisabled;

> and

> That special classes, separate schooling or other removal of children with disabilities from the regular educational environment occurs only if the nature or severity of the disability is such that education in regular classes with the use of supplementary aids and services cannot be achieved satisfactorily. (§ 300.114)

The regulations, further, support the use "of a variety of assessment tools and strategies and the gathering of relevant functional and developmental information" that will enable the student "to be involved in and progress in the general education curriculum" [34 C.F.R. 300.304(b)(ii)] and "a determination as to whether any modifications to the special education and related services are needed to enable the child to meet the annual goals set out in the IEP of the child and to participate, as appropriate, in the general curriculum" [34 C.F.R. 300.305(a)(2)(iv)].

School districts must offer a *continuum of alternative placements* to meet the needs of the children with disabilities, including instruction in general education classrooms, in special classes of schools, and home instruction; a student cannot be removed from the age-appropriate general education environment "solely because of needed modifications in the general curriculum." (34 C.F.R. 300.116)

In addition, section 300.116 now directs that the placement decision be made "in conformity with the [least restrictive environment] provisions of this subpart, including 300.114 through 300.118." The location of the child's placement must be as close as possible to the child's home with the child being educated in the school he or she would attend if nondisabled (34 C.F.R. 300.116), "unless the parent agrees otherwise" [34 C.F.R. 300.166(b)(3)]; subsection (c) of the same section reiterates that "Unless the IEP of a child with a disability requires some other arrangement, the child [is educated] in the school that he or she would attend if nondisabled, unless the parent agrees otherwise." All of the above regulations (LRE, a continuum of placements, close-to-home location, etc.) apply as well to provision of nonacademic or extracurricular services and activities (34 C.F.R. 300.117).

IEP "present levels of performance" and "measurable annual goals" (see Chapter 6) correlate to a child's involvement and progress in the general education curriculum; the "general curriculum" is defined as the "same curriculum as that for nondisabled children" [34 C.F.R. 320(a)(1)(i) and 34 C.F.R. 320(a)(2)(i)(A)]. The expectation is that the child not only will advance appropriately toward individual annual goals, but also will be involved and progress in the general curriculum, participate in extracurricular and nonacademic activities, and be educated and participate with other children with disabilities and nondisabled children in the activities described in this section [34 C.F.R. 300.320(a)(4)]. Evaluation of special education needs, related services, and supplementary aids and services should be based on peer-reviewed research to the extent possible.

The law does not say that every child with a disability has to be included in the general education classroom all the time. The presumption of the law is that a continuum of services be available for every student.

THE INCLUSION DEBATE

As mentioned earlier in this chapter, inclusion is one of the most contentious issues in special education. As noted above, federal guidelines encourage us to educate our students requiring special education services in the least restrictive environment, with their nondisabled peers. Where does the debate arise? What makes inclusion so difficult to define and implement?

Instead of framing the debate as reasons for inclusion and reasons against inclusion, it is helpful to examine the various elements and goals of inclusion and what they require on the part of the principal and school professionals—and whether these goals themselves present difficulties.

⟹ *The general education classroom is the location where the child's neighborhood peers are educated; ideally, the students all go to the same class. All students can benefit from inclusion.*

This ideal can be met only by ensuring support for all students in the class. Instruction in the general education classroom traditionally is not individualized and denies the uniqueness of the needs of students with disabilities. Special education classrooms are often more structured than general education classrooms, permitting students with disabilities a greater chance for success and improved instructional time.

⟹ *Educating students together in the general education classroom eliminates the stigma associated with removing students from the general education classroom for instruction.*

Limiting removal from the classroom during the school day ensures maximum instructional time. However, not all special education services can be provided in the general education classroom. In addition, if they are provided, they can be disruptive to the rest of the class.

⟹ *General education teachers and special education teachers use similar instructional methodologies to benefit a variety of learners.*

Unfortunately, many general education teachers and staff are not trained in how to work with students with disabilities. If students with disabilities do not receive appropriate supports, they will fall further behind their peers.

WHAT DO THE COURTS SAY?

There have been many different court cases relating to inclusion and education in the least restrictive environment. The focus of courts in different judicial circuits is varied, and might seem confusing. In some cases, the question addressed by the court is: *Can the educational services that make a segregated placement superior be provided in a nonsegregated setting?* In others, the question is: *Can education in the general education classroom with supplementary aids and services be achieved satisfactorily?*

The decisions in *Oberti v. Board of Education* (1993); *Greer v. Rome City School District*, 950 F. 2d 688, *Roncker v. Walker*, 700 F. 2d 1058 (6th Cir., 1983); and *Sacramento Unified School District v. Rachel H.*, 14 F.3d 1398 (9th Cir. 1994) that IDEA "does not permit states to make mere token gestures to accommodate handicapped students; its requirements for modifying and supplementing regular education is broad" provides guidance as to how we need to proceed.

A school district is prohibited from placing a student with disabilities outside the general education classroom if it can satisfactorily educate the child within the general education classroom with supplementary aids and support. Determining factors include the steps taken by the school to try to include the student in the general education classroom, and the comparison between the educational benefits the child would receive in each setting. Thus, a determination that a child would make greater *academic* progress in a segregated program may not warrant excluding that child from a general education classroom, given the attendant benefits of being educated with peers (e.g., social and communication skills in addition to academics). Schools are allowed to consider as well any possible negative effect inclusion may have on the education of other children in the classroom in determining the best educational setting for the child.

If placement outside of a general education classroom is necessary for the child to receive educational benefit, a school district may be violating IDEA if it has not made sufficient efforts to include the child in school programs with nondisabled children whenever possible.

Finally, a school district must consider the whole range of supplementary aids and services and must make efforts to modify the general education program to accommodate a child. If a school has not given any consideration to including the child in a general education classroom with supplementary aids and services and to modifying the general education curriculum, then it has most likely violated the IDEA directive.

WHAT IS THE BEST EDUCATIONAL SETTING?

At all times, the placement of a student with disabilities should be individualized. Many different factors help determine placement. The presumption of the law is that students with disabilities will be educated along with students without disabilities to the maximum extent appropriate. Moreover, as delineated in *Oberti*, students with disabilities should be removed from the general education classroom *only when the nature or severity of their disability prevents them from receiving an appropriate education.*

The IEP team determines the ideal placement for the student, and identifies the necessary supplementary aids and services.

WHAT IS THE PRINCIPAL'S ROLE?

The principal has the leadership role of articulating the school's (and district) policy toward providing a free appropriate education for its students with disabilities, and in ensuring that school faculty and staff are adequately prepared to support this policy. Regardless of what you feel about the inclusion of students with disabilities in the general education classrooms, the presumption of the law is that students will be educated in the least restrictive environment. There are numerous benefits for all involved. To build a cohesive teaching unit that operates in an inclusive classroom environment, you must ensure that your teaching and support staff are adequately informed and receive necessary training and support.

Step 1: Education

Is your staff familiar with the legal requirements for inclusion? Specifically, that "to the maximum extent appropriate, children with disabilities, including children in public or private institutions or other care facilities, are educated with children who are nondisabled;" and that "special classes, separate schooling or other removal of children with disabilities from the regular educational environment occurs only if the nature or severity of the disability is such that education in regular classes with the use of supplementary aids and services cannot be achieved satisfactorily." (§300.114)

This does not mean that your general education teachers will suddenly receive an influx of students with disabilities in their classrooms, without support. It does mean that your entire teaching staff must be committed to ensuring that students with disabilities receive an appropriate education. Most students with disabilities are already educated in the general education classroom most of the time, many of these students have mild disabilities that are not immediately apparent.

Many students with more severe disabilities have historically been included in almost all noncurricular activities (such as lunch, art, music, recess, and traveling to and from the school). Students with disabilities often do much better in structured activities. You are now working to integrate them into structured academic activities, and it is a team effort.

Some students have behaviors or needs so different from the other students that they will need assistance outside of the general education classroom. However, they should be serviced outside the general education classroom only after a concerted effort to meet their needs with supplementary aids and services.

Step 2: Support

Are you fully supporting your teachers' needs in implementing inclusion at your school? You need to ensure that your class compositions reflect "natural proportions." This means that students with disabilities are in classrooms with other students in the same or natural proportions of the general population. (For example, the prevalence rate for students with learning disabilities is that of 5–6% of the total population. Therefore, you would work to keep the proportion of students with learning disabilities in a general education classroom of about 5–6%, or in a class of 20, about one or two students.)

Are your general education teachers familiar with appropriate classroom modifications and accommodations (as mentioned in the Introduction and described in Chapter 5? Have you made an effort to ensure that your special education staff and general education staff work together (see Chapter 2)?

Do not overburden the same teachers with potential problems every semester. Plan with the teachers who will work with specific students, and how the teachers will work together to meet the students' needs.

Step 3: Time

All students have needs that change over the course of the school year. Individuals who are working to meet those needs require opportunities to plan and work together to adapt to changes. Teacher schedules (see Chapters 1 and 2) should include regularly scheduled meeting times for teachers to work, to plan, and to reflect on current concerns and situations. Ideally, there would be time for this each day, but it is perhaps more practical to reserve time once a week. Even 20 to 30 dedicated minutes a week can help address problem situations, and prevent problems from getting out of hand.

You need to make a personal time commitment in order to develop and implement a successful inclusion program that benefits all students. You need to allot time for yourself and for your teachers not only for planning, but also for inservice programs and attending professional association conferences and meetings.

Inservice programs help teachers learn more about their profession, as it applies to the unique students in your school. What do your teachers want to know about working with students with disabilities? Find someone who can talk with your staff about successful processes; it's especially helpful if your expert can return to your school to respond to implementation questions a month or two after first meeting with your staff. Your own teams of teachers and staff can also help strategize and problem-solve, as well as identify what additional information is needed to help solve certain problems.

Conferences and meetings allow your staff to learn more about the latest trends in the field; they can visit with other teachers who are trying to solve similar problems and hear what happens in other districts. Too often, it is just special education teachers attending conferences relating to students with disabilities. All of your teaching staff needs information about the latest changes and to be provided the opportunity to share ideas.

Step 4: Commitment

The most important thing about working with students with disabilities in your school is a concerted commitment to work to provide for their education. You are the principal of ALL the students. You demonstrate your commitment by attending and participating in IEP meetings, asking questions about how students are doing, reinforcing positives when students with disabilities are working effectively, and reinforcing positives when special education teachers and other staff are working together to meet the needs of students with disabilities.

8

What Does a Principal Need to Know About Discipline of Students With Disabilities?

KEVIN KOURY AND KATHERINE MITCHEM

Principals are responsible for enforcing discipline for all students and maintaining a safe school environment. Given recent media events and societal issues, principals must respond immediately to inappropriate student behaviors that disrupt the learning environment and/or pose psychological or physical harm to others. In addition, it is the principal's responsibility to ensure that drugs and weapons are not brought onto school premises. If a drug or weapons violation occurs, principals are responsible for reporting this to law enforcement agencies. Fortunately, there are promising practices, student supports, and program options available to help principals maintain a safe school environment, deter inappropriate behavior, and support the needs of students with disabilities.

THE CURRENT ENVIRONMENT

Many states are adopting safe school curricular program options, affective curriculums, and mental health services within schools. Many of these changes have some research support for their effectiveness in deterring aggression and promoting appropriate behavior, and more continues to be learned about effective methods of achieving these goals.

Many schools and law enforcement agencies have initiated *collaborative relationships* outlining details and procedures for crisis situations. These collaborative relationships involve (a) generating plans for dealing with crises immediately, (b) instituting procedures for identifying early warning signs of a crisis, and (c) establishing a course of action when a crisis is imminent. The collaborative effort seeks to establish a proactive preventive model for maintaining safe schools.

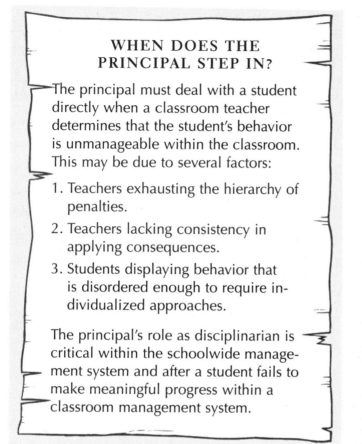

WHEN DOES THE PRINCIPAL STEP IN?

The principal must deal with a student directly when a classroom teacher determines that the student's behavior is unmanageable within the classroom. This may be due to several factors:

1. Teachers exhausting the hierarchy of penalties.

2. Teachers lacking consistency in applying consequences.

3. Students displaying behavior that is disordered enough to require individualized approaches.

The principal's role as disciplinarian is critical within the schoolwide management system and after a student fails to make meaningful progress within a classroom management system.

The principal should have a variety of disciplinary options beyond simple procedures (such as suspension or expulsion) to meet the challenges of maintaining a safe school. These options should be part of a schoolwide framework where the principal also maintains and protects the rights of the entire school.

GOVERNING REGULATIONS

Within the operating framework, the principal needs to know the federal and state laws governing the education of students with disabilities. For the first time in special education history, addressing behavior was recognized in the 1997 Amendments to the Individuals with Disabilities Education Act (IDEA '97) as part of providing a free and appropriate education. The law specified certain services and procedures that must be used in disciplining students who are receiving special education services.

The 2004 Individuals with Disabilities Education Improvement Act (IDEIA) made some changes to the provisions of IDEA regarding discipline, but continues to demonstrate a commitment to addressing the problem behaviors of students. The states also have their own requirements for establishing, implementing, and evaluating school discipline. Principals have the responsibility of ensuring that these requirements are met in their schools in ways that meet the needs of the students in question and the school as a whole.

MANAGING STUDENT BEHAVIOR

To a large extent, the principal depends first upon teachers to manage their students' behavior.

Typically, teachers design their own management systems in the form of stated and posted rules with accompanying consequences, penalties, or punishment for rule infractions. Other discipline systems and techniques encourage positive behavior by "catching students being good" and then recognizing them for their good behavior. However, the positive component may not be addressed consistently in many classroom management plans.

IDEIA (2004) mandates that behavioral intervention be positive in nature. Recently, some classrooms and entire schools have incorporated systems of positive reinforcement for group or individual demonstration of desirable behavior. Behavior management systems that focus only on rewarding appropriate behavior fall short of providing true positive behavior support for students. Good behavior management systems should support the student and teach appropriate replacement behaviors in conjunction with shaping appropriate behavior patterns.

Sometimes schools develop more global approaches using an adapted or modified classroom system that makes the principal responsible for implementation. The principal should take an active part in any plan developed to ensure that it complies with federal and state policies. The development of a schoolwide system of behavior management may require the principal to initiate collaboration among various school personnel to ensure that the system includes a variety of interventions and preventative features. A schoolwide discipline policy consisting merely of removal procedures will not meet the school's needs or the requirements of IDEIA (2004).

IDEA AND ASSOCIATED POLICY

The principal must be aware of how administration of any schoolwide or individualized plan of action regarding a student's behavior may be considered a violation of IDEIA (2004). First, the principal is required to administer discipline according to the components of the individualized education program (IEP) if there are behavior stipulations. The social, emotional, and behavioral needs of students with disabilities vary greatly. Many students with disabilities receive appropriate support through the classroom management system and the schoolwide discipline system.

Occasionally, however, students with disabilities require individualized behavioral support going beyond components outlined within classroom and schoolwide systems. Therefore, the principal must examine the stipulations and supports delineated within the IEP to maintain a free, appropriate public education (FAPE). Under IDEA '97, when the suspension or expulsion of a student with an IEP was considered, the principal had to make sure that certain requirements of IDEA '97 were met; with the reauthorization of IDEIA (2004), some of these requirements have changed (see Table 8-1). States and school districts have guidelines for adhering to these requirements, based on the federal regulations.

The principal's expertise regarding discipline systems within the school should become a resource not only when behavioral problems occur, but also during the IEP planning stage. An informed principal can help design positive behavior supports that align and integrate the existing behavior expectations within the school, and assimilate the program into existing supports within the school.

The school principal has a unilateral disciplinary option when a student with a disability misbehaves and the misbehavior warrants removal from the school.

Suspension can be used as an option even when the misbehavior is related to a student's disability.

TABLE 8-1. CHANGES TO DISCIPLINE PROVISIONS FROM IDEA 1997 TO IDEIA 2004

IDEA (1997)	IDEIA (2004)
No student with a disability can be denied continuing educational services due to behavior. Schools must continue to provide educational services for students with disabilities whose suspension or expulsion constitutes a change in placement (usually more than 10 days in a school year). Schools have the authority to remove students with disabilities to appropriate interim alternative educational settings (IAES) for behavior related to drugs, guns, and other dangerous weapons for up to 45 days.	School personnel may consider any unique circumstances on a case-by-case basis when determining whether to order a change in placement for a child with a disability who violates a code of student conduct. [615(k)(1)(A)] In addition to the old standard allowing removal for drugs, guns, and other dangerous weapons, a new standard is established for special circumstances. Schools may remove a student to an interim alternative educational setting for up to 45 school days without regard to whether the behavior is determined to be a manifestation of the child's disability in cases where the student "has inflicted serious bodily injury upon another person while at school, on school premises, or at a school function under the jurisdiction of the SEA or LEA." [615(k)(1)(G)]
Schools are permitted to suspend students with disabilities for up to 10 school days to the extent that such alternatives are used for children without disabilities.	
The IEP team is required to conduct a "manifestation determination" once disciplinary action for a student with a disability is contemplated. The IEP team must determine—within 10 calendar days after the school decides to discipline a student—whether the student's behavior is related to the disability. If the behavior is not related to the disability, the student may be disciplined in the same way as a student without a disability, but the appropriate educational services must continue.	The reauthorization also establishes a new standard for manifestation determination. Within 10 school days of any decision to change the placement of a child with a disability because of a violation of a code of student conduct, the local education agency, the parent, and relevant members of the IEP team (as determined by the parent and the LEA) must review all relevant information in the student's file, including the child's IEP, any teacher observations, and any relevant information provided by the parents to determine if the conduct in question was:

continues

TABLE 8-1. CONTINUED

IDEA (1997)	IDEIA (2004)
	✓ Caused by, or had a direct and substantial relationship to, the child's disability; or
	✓ The direct result of the LEA's failure to implement the IEP.
	✓ If there is a determination that a behavior was a manifestation of the disability, the IEP team must
	✓ Conduct a functional behavioral assessment and implement a behavioral intervention plan for the student, if this had not been done prior to the behavior that resulted in the change in placement.
	✓ Review the plan where one exists and modify it as necessary to address the behavior
	✓ Except for safe school violations described above, return the student to the placement from which he or she was removed unless the parent and LEA agree to a change of placement as part of the modification of the behavior intervention plan.
School personnel are permitted to report crimes allegedly committed by students with disabilities to law enforcement authorities	

However, it is very important to adhere to the limits at the principal's discretion. During the school year, a principal must not exceed the 10-day limit of removal of a student with disabilities. The 10-day rule affords the principal discretion to administer schoolwide discipline to all students equally. The principal must grant a student with disabilities the same rights granted any student without disabilities during short-term suspension periods. Therefore, it might be wise to develop a system wherein the 10-day period would be enough to span the entire school year (i.e., reduce the suspension time intervals to shorter periods and required parental and/or professional input).

Change of Placement and Interim Alternative Setting

When the cumulative total of days a student with disabilities is removed from school reaches 10, further removal is considered a *change of placement*. This can be accomplished only by reconvening the IEP team to consider the change of placement. In order for principals to maintain a consistent disciplinary approach for all students, they may choose to limit school suspensions for all students to the 10-day limit.

One nuance in IDEIA (2004) regards the time period for removal to an *interim alternative setting*. When a change of placement meeting is necessary, the school now has a period of up to 45 school days rather 45 calendar days to use an interim alternative setting. As stated previously, all components of the IEP must be continued in this placement, and the behavior that initiated the removal becomes the focus of the IEP committee efforts to address the specific behaviors related to the student's removal. Specific behaviors requiring removal to an appropriate interim alternative educational setting are mentioned in IDEA.

The principal is authorized to remove a student with disabilities from the school for behavioral reasons. However, the removal of students with disabilities must be consistent with the practice of removing students without disabilities; the removal must include assignment to an appropriate interim alternative educational placement; and the removal must not exceed 45 school days. Student behavior that constitutes cause for the removal includes (a) bringing a weapon to school; (b) possessing, distributing, or selling drugs or other controlled substances at school or a sanctioned school function; and (c) inflicting serious bodily injury on another person while on school grounds or at a school function [615(k)(1)(G)].

Placement in an appropriate interim alternative educational setting is also permitted if, after a due process hearing, a student has been determined to be a danger to self or others. In all cases, this placement may continue for an additional 45 school days if it is requested, there is no objection, and it is determined to be the best placement due to circumstances surrounding the individual student. If the local education agency (LEA; i.e., the school) believes the student would be dangerous to himself or others if returned to the original setting, the process is repeatable. As always, all parties are entitled to the due process hearing.

Functional Behavioral Assessment and Behavioral Intervention Support Plan

After an appropriate interim alternative educational placement has been decided upon, the school must complete a functional behavioral assessment within 10 business days. The guidelines to be considered include information regarding schoolwide efforts to minimize the threat within the current placement as well as the appropriateness of the interim placement to provide FAPE. There must be access to the general curriculum as stipulated in the IEP and provision of an environment conducive to accomplishing goals set forth in the student's existing, modified, or new behavioral intervention plan.

The functional behavioral assessment is used to plan and then implement behavioral intervention supports for the student with disabilities.

The behavioral intervention support plan, when developed by the team, becomes part of the student's IEP.

As a component of the IEP, this plan must be in compliance with all requirements of IDEIA. Any action by the principal that may be considered a change of placement requires reconvening the IEP team to establish the correct placement for the student.

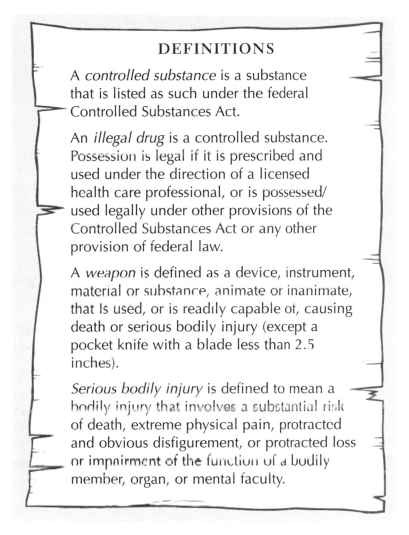

DEFINITIONS

A *controlled substance* is a substance that is listed as such under the federal Controlled Substances Act.

An *illegal drug* is a controlled substance. Possession is legal if it is prescribed and used under the direction of a licensed health care professional, or is possessed/used legally under other provisions of the Controlled Substances Act or any other provision of federal law.

A *weapon* is defined as a device, instrument, material or substance, animate or inanimate, that is used, or is readily capable of, causing death or serious bodily injury (except a pocket knife with a blade less than 2.5 inches).

Serious bodily injury is defined to mean a bodily injury that involves a substantial risk of death, extreme physical pain, protracted and obvious disfigurement, or protracted loss or impairment of the function of a bodily member, organ, or mental faculty.

The principal should ensure that a behavioral support intervention plan is in the IEP and in place for any student removed to an interim placement. If the student already has a behavioral support intervention plan, then the IEP team must reconvene to analyze the appropriateness of the plan, along with its implementation, in light of the behavior that resulted in the student's removal. After the plan is evaluated and implemented, the team must modify or adjust it to meet the needs created by the misconduct, the new alternative interim placement, or events leading to the action resulting in the student's removal.

Principals need to understand that the IDEA reauthorization in 2004 enables administration of schoolwide discipline plans, including options for immediate response to crises involving drugs, weapons, or danger of physical harm. The law is constructed to ensure proper administration and maintenance of a safe school environment. An effective schoolwide discipline plan should be designed to comply with the provisions of IDEIA, allow for positive behavioral supports, administer sanctions equally and without excess, and ensure a safe learning environment for all students.

When removal to an appropriate alternative interim educational placement is under consideration, the appropriateness of the student's current placement is to be considered. Information regarding the school's efforts to minimize the threat within the current placement (a function of an effective schoolwide discipline plan) also must be considered, as well as the appropriateness of the interim placement to provide FAPE. There must be access to the general curriculum as stipulated in the IEP, as well as provision of an environment conducive to accomplishing goals set forth in the student's existing, modified, or new behavioral intervention plan.

When collecting data and information, the principal should be aware that anecdotal records are a necessary source of information, but are not alone sufficient to support removal of a student to an appropriate alternative interim placement. The school principal has a distinct role in maintaining records, documenting incidents, and initiating appropriate evaluations and observations from a variety of sources. These records become important when the due process hearing officer makes an informed determination.

The principal must be able to provide to any person, including a hearing officer, assurance that (a) the IEP is appropriate and (b) all components of the IEP were implemented as prescribed. It is important to maintain data concerning progress toward goals contained in the IEP. In addition, the data must verify that all related services were provided as prescribed in the IEP and that the behavioral intervention plan, if there was one, was appropriate and implemented as prescribed in the IEP. Finally, the principal may not act unilaterally regarding where to place the student in the interim; the IEP team is responsible for selecting the alternative educational setting of a child with disabilities.

When contemplating removal, it is the principal's responsibility to notify the parents, advising them of the school's intentions and their rights. This allows the parents, the IEP team, and all other involved parties to determine whether or not the behavior in question was caused by, or had a direct and substantial relationship to, the student's disability; or was the direct result of the school's failure to implement the IEP. This is a *manifestation determination* meeting; it must occur within 10 school days of any decision to change the placement of a student with a disability.

Manifestation Determination Review

Manifestation determination review is a mechanism requiring all parties to review events of school rule infractions or misconduct (cumulative 10-day rule), a weapons violation, or a drug/controlled substance violation for the purpose of determining whether the infraction is a result of the student's disability. The findings of this determination will be that the behavior subject to the disciplinary action either is or is not a result or a manifestation of the student's disability. In making this determination, the team may use a form (see Appendix 8A) to review and consider all information available, including all evaluation and diagnostics results (including what the parent provides), all observations of the child, and all components of the IEP as well as the educational placement.

After reviewing all available information, the team determines whether the IEP was appropriate and implemented correctly according to all components stipulated, or whether the conduct in question was caused by, or had a direct and substantial relationship to the student's disability.

If, after the review, the manifestation determination team concludes that the IEP was deficient or not implemented according to prescription, then the school must take actions to remedy the situation. However, if the team finds that the school did comply, the team may determine that the behavior subject to disciplinary action was not a manifestation of the student's disability. If that is the team's finding, the student is subject to the conditions of discipline set forth in the school's code of conduct. However, before this happens, one additional requirement must be met: The student's disciplinary records must be forwarded to the person(s) who will administer the school discipline. A student's parents may always request a due process hearing to challenge the results, findings, or rulings of the manifestation determination team. The "stay-put" rule for placement before the interim alternative educational placement is in effect throughout the due process hearing period unless the student is a danger to self or others.

The due process hearing must be conducted within 20 school days of request, and result in a determination within 10 days of the hearing.

Recordkeeping

Principals must maintain records of poor behavior for all students in the school. This information is important, because a part of the law regarding students with disabilities concerns whether the school has knowledge that a student is currently unidentified but requires special services. A student who may be identified in the future for special education services, or who has a history of poor behavior and is documented in a variety of ways, is protected if they are subsequently found to be a student with a disability. When this student is identified, the administration of discipline as a general education student without disabilities no longer applies, and the student falls under IDEIA guidelines. This standard is more commonly known as the "previous knowledge of a disability" section of the 1997 Amendments to IDEA and was revised in IDEIA 2004.

If no previous knowledge exists, if the parent has not allowed an evaluation, and/or the LEA previously conducted assessment for eligibility and found the student not eligible, or determined that assessment was not necessary and provided just reason to

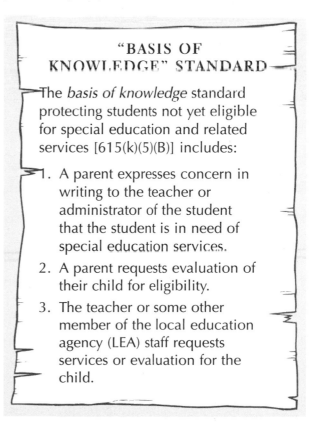

"BASIS OF KNOWLEDGE" STANDARD

The *basis of knowledge* standard protecting students not yet eligible for special education and related services [615(k)(5)(B)] includes:

1. A parent expresses concern in writing to the teacher or administrator of the student that the student is in need of special education services.
2. A parent requests evaluation of their child for eligibility.
3. The teacher or some other member of the local education agency (LEA) staff requests services or evaluation for the child.

the parents for not conducting an assessment for eligibility, then previous knowledge is present but has been disposed correctly. In this case, the student is subject to the same administration of discipline as a student without disabilities. In any event, parents may request an evaluation, and if they do, an expedited due process hearing is required. If, as a result of the evaluation, the student is determined to be eligible for special education services, then special education services are to be provided to the student by the LEA, and placement, curriculum, and service decisions become part of the IEP team's responsibility.

The principal should be aware of the timeline established for expedited due process hearings in the state and local education agencies. In general, all requested due process hearings under IDEIA (2004) and accompanying federal policy require decisions and dissemination of decisions within 45 days of the request for the hearing. However, expedited hearings regarding interim alternative educational settings are governed by the 20-day hearing and 10-day decision rules previously described.

If a student with a disability commits a crime, the LEA is not restricted by IDEIA from reporting the crime to the proper local, state, or federal enforcement agencies. There is no prohibitive aspect of IDEIA regarding any law enforcement agency from enforcing local, state, or federal law. The agency reporting a crime may transmit special education and disciplinary records of students with disabilities to law enforcement agencies for their consideration, but they may not breach any Family Educational Rights and Privacy Act (FERPA) provisions (see Chapter 3). This is similar to the establishment of the new placement or authority to administer discipline when a "no manifestation of disability" is reached.

Although a student with a disability can be excluded from his or her current educational placement, at no time can the LEA cease services or the provision of FAPE.

The LEA (including the principal) must demonstrate participation in the IEP process and the creation of an appropriate IEP. More important, the LEA is required to implement the IEP as prescribed and document student progress toward the goals and objectives established in the IEP.

THE SCHOOLWIDE DISCIPLINE PLAN

As mentioned previously, the principal needs to be the administrative leader of the schoolwide discipline plan. The schoolwide plan should have a number of ways to identify students who need behavioral support, the behaviors they exhibit, the frequency with which and the conditions under which these behaviors occur as well as the benefits or payoff that the student derives from the behavior. This requires a system of recording and documenting, which in turn necessitates skilled observers who are trained to record events, interviews with participants (including parents), identification of problem behaviors, and determination of events leading to and subsequent to occurrences of problem behavior. The schoolwide plan should also serve all students equally, thus requiring consistent application and administration of the schoolwide plan. The principal's role within the construct of the IEP committee should serve to help all members fully understand the behavioral expectations and supports within the school. However, specific mechanisms must be in place to identify behavioral excesses, deficits, and support needs of individual students. The school should be prepared to explore the behavioral needs of the student through various behavioral identification and analysis processes.

Behavioral Identification

Office discipline referrals are often the first data that an administrator considers when reviewing the schoolwide discipline plan. A well-defined schoolwide discipline plan has a data-collection system that is comprehensive and helps to validate behaviors. In this type of situation, these data can help school personnel identify "hot spots" in the school that call for a review of schoolwide expectations or increased monitoring, as well as individual "frequent flyers" who may be in need of more intensive and individualized behavior supports. The schoolwide discipline recordkeeping system will have a set of data-collection instruments such as detention slips, office referral slips, observation forms such as fixed-interval time sampling forms, and incident reports. One skill that should be the focus of inservice training for teachers is the accurate and consistent completion of narrative data-collection instruments. This skill is very important to ensure that the behavior described is clear, measurable, and understandable, as well as critical for success.

It is particularly important when recording behavior incidents to be sure to describe the behavior so that a stranger could understand the behavior and to be sure that the behavior is sufficiently important to warrant this attention. An incident report (see Appendix 8B) used for reporting this information should describe the following:

1. What was happening just before the incident.

2. What the student was doing before the incident.

3. What was said or done to the student.

4. Details of what happened throughout the incident.

5. What happened (consequences) immediately after the incident.

Other data necessary on the form include the student's name, date, time of day, location of the incident, who was present, and who completed the incident report. Summarizing these data on a regular basis (at least monthly) allows school personnel to identify which students are offending most frequently, what they are doing, when they are doing it, and where the behaviors are occurring. This information is invaluable to the administrator who wants to address discipline issues strategically and use the least resources necessary to do so.

In addition to schoolwide data, teachers may keep anecdotal notes regarding incidents of poor behavior. For students who, despite schoolwide supports, need more intensive intervention, anecdotal notes from teachers—as well as the use of a behavior checklist—may be indicated.

Behavior Checklists

Behavior checklists (see Table 8-2) afford the opportunity to gather specific behavioral information from a variety of people who know the student best and have observed the student's behavior. Generally, behavior checklists are used to identify the poor behavior(s) or problem behavior(s) a student exhibits and record how often they occur.

TABLE 8-2. EXAMPLES OF PROBLEM BEHAVIOR CHECKLISTS AND PUBLISHERS

BEHAVIOR CHECKLIST	PUBLISHER
The Behavior Evaluation Scale - 2 (BES-3:L)	Hawthorne
The Emotional Behavior Disorders Scale (EBDS-R)	Hawthorne
The Attention Deficit Disorders Evaluation Scale (ADDES-3)	Hawthorne
The Behavior Rating Profile (BRP-2)	Pro-Ed
The Social Skills Rating System (SSRS)	AGS

Behavior checklists are just one component of a data-collection system for determining a behavioral support program for a student. However, they are a good step in identifying behaviors that need to be addressed in the school.

Faculty and staff need to be aware of the instruments available in the school, know how to complete the checklists, and understand the scoring. To enhance consistency in use and scoring, it would be best to introduce these assessment instruments to teachers and staff at an inservice training session at the time a schoolwide behavior plan is implemented. Follow-up training will probably be needed as problems occur and when there are staff changes.

The BES-2, EBDS, and ADDES each have a variety of versions. It is important to note each of these instruments describes only inappropriate behaviors. All of these instruments request the rater to provide his or her interpretation of the frequency with which the poor behavior occurs. The ranges of the rating scales for the instruments are from *never occurring* to *occurring continuously throughout the day*. Subjectivity of rating is evident and depends on the ability of the rater to understand the type of scale and its rating system. There are unique aspects, both positive and negative, of each of the scales listed.

The principal must exercise caution when collecting behavior ratings, checklists, and other recorded data, because it becomes very easy to focus on the problem rather than developing positive behavioral supports for the student when poor behavior is identified. Behavioral checklists are tools to use to help meet the student's needs, and should not be misused to serve the needs of others (i.e., to serve as documentation of a problem severe enough to justify removal from the general education environment). An important aspect of behavior intervention and support is that of creating the most supportive environment to facilitate student success.

When collecting assessment data on a student's problem behaviors, the principal should be aware that previous knowledge is documented and ensure that this results in positive action regarding a student and his or her overall educational program. While behavioral data collected from a variety of sources are necessary and can provide information needed to begin a behavioral support program, they are not a sufficient source of information for creating effective behavioral support programs. Once target behaviors are identified, the next step is to analyze the learning situation and environment to determine why the behavior(s) occur.

Once all data are collected, the IEP committee is ready to begin to determine the function a behavior has for the student. This requires a functional behavioral assessment using the data about a student's problem behavior as well as other information gathered through observation, records, new information, and interviews.

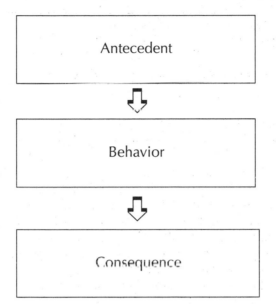

FIGURE 8-1. VARIABLES IN FUNCTIONAL
BEHAVIORAL ASSESSMENT

Functional Behavioral Assessment

Functional behavioral assessment is required as a part of the process for
establishing a behavior support plan.

Functional behavioral assessment is based on information about how a student may
react to certain situations and analysis of the functions the problem behaviors serve for
the student—the relationship between the student's behavior and what occurs as a
result of that behavior. This provides information to the team about how situations
may be adjusted, changed, or manipulated so that a problem behavior no longer exists
or can no longer occur. Sources of information include the home, classroom, and
community.

    What can be manipulated varies as well, since sometimes the events leading to
the behavior (antecedents) may be removed. The student may be trained to exhibit an
appropriate behavior to replace the undesirable behavior (behavior), or the desired
consequence may be changed to interrupt the functional relationship to the behavior
(consequence). (See Figure 8-1.)

    Antecedents (A) may or may not be under the control of the teacher or another
authority figure. Consequences (C) also may be within the control of the teacher, principal, or other authority in the school. The behavior (B) can be adjusted, but this takes
planning and training for those involved. Problems can be minimized through the systematic collection of information and data using an A-B-C recording chart. The functional assessment after the observation of the antecedent, behavior, and consequence
(i.e., A-B-C chart analysis) clarifies the course of action to be taken by authority or student, and how that may take place.

Jerry, a 10th grade student at Utopia High School, has received a series of office referrals from a number of teachers for disrespect, noncompliance, and blatant refusal to complete work. In each instance, teachers have typically made an office referral and requested that the student be excluded from class for an additional day.

When the principal reviews the incident reports, he notices that the referrals typically occur at the end of the day and when extensive independent reading and writing activities are assigned. The principal is aware that the student has a learning disability. In most of the narrative descriptions there appears to be escalation of events that occurs prior to the removal that leads to the removal.

What might be contributing to this situation?

- Teacher tolerance.
- Tedious/challenging work assignments.
- Student avoidance of work, the teacher, and/or classmates.
- Removal of the student may be negatively reinforcing both the student (escape from the aversive environment) and the teacher (avoidance of the aversive student).

In this situation, the principal needs to analyze the facts and continue data collection by interviewing the student at the time of removal to generate a student incident report. Comparing the student and teacher incident reports may allow the principal to determine possible antecedents to and functions of the behaviors. Finally, the principal gathers the players (those involved) to develop an intervention plan that includes manipulation of antecedents and consequences as well as teaching alternative replacement behaviors to stabilize the learning environment.

For example, in this situation, the teachers may agree to alter either the schedule of when the independent reading activity is assigned or the format of the assignment so that it is less challenging for the student. In addition, the student may be taught to request assistance as well as perhaps requesting a short break from the assignment to get a drink of water. Providing the student access to brief escape or assistance may prevent the student from escalating his behavior in order to be removed completely from the class.

Consequating inappropriate behavior without teaching appropriate replacement behaviors may be considered a denial of FAPE.

Implementing and evaluating behavior intervention plans such as this assists principals in providing students with disabilities FAPE as well as promoting a safe and productive learning environment for all students.

Individualized Intervention

The functional behavioral assessment is required to begin developing an individualized intervention for a student who displays challenging behavior(s). Sometimes when schools use a particular inflexible consequence for unacceptable behavior, certain students become chronic offenders. A *consequence* generally is used to reduce behavior (i.e., punish), yet some students repeatedly break rules and suffer the same consequences. The functional behavioral assessment can reveal whether a repeat offender is *reinforced* by the consequence. For example, suspending a student who has received repeated suspensions for disrespect in the classroom is likely to be considered a sanctioned vacation day by the student rather than the punishment the administrator intended.

The principal should be aware of many sources of information that can become a part of the functional behavioral assessment. Individuals, collecting and analyzing information as a part of functional behavioral assessment, need training to collect data and analyze them effectively. The principal can provide this through inservice training in the school.

The first step is *identifying existing problematic behaviors*. This can be accomplished by using some kind of norm-referenced, easy to score assessment instrument to identify specific problematic behaviors and verify that they are sufficient to warrant intervention. These formal assessments establish sources of information from the school, home, community, and the student (see Table 8-2).

Next, further *analyze the identified behaviors* and their associated problems using some type of observation system. The observation should be designed to obtain information about the student within the environment that the behavior occurs and compare that performance to the performance of peers in the same classroom, hallway, cafeteria, and so forth, thereby establishing an existing norm. This allows including data about variance in teacher tolerance and teaching practice as a part of the evaluative process. These factors together help the team determine how the learning community supports or abandons a particular student and subsequently can assure that no student is abandoned.

For example, classroom observation of the target student's behavior can be compared to the norm established in that classroom by alternating observations of other classmates with observations of the target student. Collecting such data helps establish the behavioral performance of the norm (in this case, the classroom as a whole). Then the analysis can be comparative, and a student's performance has a benchmark for setting goals. What you may find, however, is that the target student's behavior is similar to that of the class as a whole, thus suggesting that teacher tolerance of the individual student is a factor rather than the behavior itself.

The relationship between behavior and consequence can be found to be functional for the student; that is, the student is reinforced by the consequence we consider to be punishment.

Another source of information that should be considered during the functional assessment is the *recorded data* from the schoolwide discipline program. These data will be in the actual forms used in the school to record specific incidents of behavior, frequency of detention referrals, and frequency of principal referrals. In all cases, the principal is the one person in the school with an overall working understanding of each set of a student's behavior data. That information, if recorded according to guidelines described previously, becomes a valuable resource for planning an individual student's behavioral support intervention plan.

The principal now is in the position of helping the team establish a plan for the student who needs behavioral support and can ensure that the plan is functional and fits the overall schoolwide discipline plan.

POSITIVE BEHAVIOR SUPPORT SYSTEMS

To be successful, positive behavioral support approaches should follow a set of steps:

1. Identifying behaviors that need to be changed.
2. Identifying antecedents to the behavior and determining how to alter these so that the behavior no longer occurs and is thus irrelevant to the student.
3. Identifying the function of the student's behavior and determining an appropriate, functional replacement behavior.
4. Determining effective consequences for appropriate and inappropriate behaviors.
5. Establishing a reinforcement schedule.
6. Verifying successful results through a system of data collection.

Reinforcement is a process that strengthens the behavior that precedes it. When selecting reinforcement, it is important for the principal and teachers to remember that the purpose of reinforcement here is to strengthen appropriate behavior, not problem behavior. For this reason, it is important to monitor reactions to see whether a reinforcing consequence has indeed been selected and applied contingent on appropriate behavior. In addition, students may become satiated on a particular reinforcer so it is important to vary the reinforcers available to the student.

The teacher can conduct a *reinforcement survey* to help determine preferred reinforcement for students who need positive behavior support. In general, this is a forced-choice questionnaire comparing reinforcement categorized into five hierarchical levels. The five levels of reinforcement move along a continuum from extrinsic (e.g., praise or a reward from another person) to intrinsic (e.g., satisfaction at knowing you did a good job). The categories range from edibles (extrinsic), to concrete items, to free-time activities, to gaining peer approval, and finally to getting teacher recognition (intrinsic). A survey of this type has 40 items of paired-reinforcement suggestions comparing the different types of reinforcement to each other an equal number of times. This enables the assessor to determine the most preferred reinforcement type for the student.

In creating the questionnaire one must be sure to have an understanding of edible reinforcement, concrete reinforcement, free-time activities, peer approval opportunities and specific types of teacher recognition the student would prefer. Caution is advised when using edibles, for a number of reasons (e.g., candy would be inappropriate for a child with diabetes, or parents may not wish their child to have certain edibles). Concrete items should be affordable for the teacher(s) and/or principal, since they will probably have to supply these with their own money.

The age and grade level of the student should be incorporated in the list of possible reinforcement items to be considered on the survey. Observing what students enjoy doing in their free time is another option in terms of identifying possible reinforcers for students. One suggestion is to create surveys for a school that can be adjusted according to the unique needs of students, their ages, and the teacher's willingness to provide certain types of reinforcement.

THE PRINCIPAL'S ROLE IN EFFECTIVE DISCIPLINE

The principal can be proactive and support teaching practice that is academically sound and motivating. Teachers need to provide constant monitoring and maintain classroom awareness. For positive behavioral supports to be effective, it is vital to ensure that behaviors are defined correctly, that the function the behavior provides to the student is understood, and that reinforcers of replacement behaviors are acceptable and appropriate.

A team approach is necessary to develop an effective program at the school level that enhances classroom management and provides administrative support. Discipline committees consisting of representatives from general education and special education, principals, parents, and the student population are helpful to ensure a thorough understanding of behavioral expectations and consistency in responding to various behavioral concerns.

APPENDIX 8A

MANIFESTATION DETERMINATION INFORMATIONAL REPORT

Student Name: _____ Date: _____

School: _____

I. Disability Conditions (Indicate all sources as well as information.)

Evaluation and Diagnostic Reports

Information Supplied by the Parents

Observations

Student's IEP/Placement

Supplemental Aids and Services Provided

Discipline Records

Cumulative Records

Teacher Documentation

Police/Incident Records

New Assessment Data

Other Information

II. Describe the proposed disciplinary action:

III. Behavioral History

Effectiveness of Previous Interventions

History of Current Behavior Subject to Disciplinary Action

Behaviors Addressed in the IEP or Other Behavior Intervention Plans

Have the Behavior Intervention Plans Been Implemented?

Were There Any Changes in Behavior?

Other Comments Regarding Behavior Interventions Plans

IV. Review of Past Evaluations

History of Disability (or Disabilities)

Consistency of Evaluations With Current Behavior

Other

V. Summary of New Data Collected

Precise Description of Disability

Consistency With Previous Evaluation Data

Summary of Results

MANIFESTATION DETERMINATION CHECKLIST AND WORKSHEET

Attach a description of the incident. (Provide details, documentation; secure voluntary statements from parents, the child, and individuals involved.)

___Yes   ___No   Are there previous Manifestation Determination decisions for this student?

Individualized Education Program (IEP) Evaluation

___Yes   ___No   1.   At the time of the incident, did the student have a disability? (If no, go to item 12.)

___Yes   ___No   2.   Is the entire IEP team present?

___Yes   ___No   3.   Is a parent of the child present?

                   4.   List other qualified personnel present.

_____

_____

_____

___Yes   ___No   5.   Are all required IEP components available? (If no, indicate what is missing.)

___Yes   ___No   6.   Were all educational needs of the student addressed in the IEP? (If no, indicate which student needs are missing.)

_____

_____

_____

___Yes   ___No   7.   Was positive behavioral support included in the IEP?

___Yes   ___No   If yes, were goals and objectives appropriate and was progress documented?

___Yes   ___No   If no, does the IEP address all behavioral needs of this student?

___Yes   ___No   8.   Were all of the following items considered when creating the IEP?

___Yes   ___No   • Behavioral interventions/strategies for behavior that impedes learning

___Yes   ___No   • Language needs

___Yes   ___No   • Communication needs

___Yes   ___No   • Assistive technology needs

___Yes   ___No   • Needs for blind or visually impaired

___Yes   ___No   9.   Is the educational placement in the IEP appropriate for this student? (If no, provide rationale from IEP, who disagrees, and why.)

_____

_____

_____

___Yes   ___No   10.   Were all diagnostic/evaluation results considered when constructing the IEP? (If no, indicate which results were not considered and why.)

_____

_____

___Yes   ___No   11.   Were all prescribed supplementary aids and services provided? (If no, indicate which supplementary aids or services are lacking.)

_____

_____

___Yes   ___No   12.   Is there previous knowledge of behavioral problems? (If yes, document in chronological order the specific behaviors, extent of behaviors, and disciplinary actions to date. Indicate sources of information.)

_____

_____

_____

___Yes   ___No   13.   Do these behaviors require intervention? (If yes, explain/discuss possible interventions.)

_____

_____

_____

___Yes   ___No   14.   Is diagnostic/evaluation information missing? (If yes, indicate the new information and its source. Items to consider include individual specialist's reports, multidisciplinary team reports, current parent/teacher information, anecdotal records of behavior, documentation and cumulative history of behavior, the context where behavior occurs, student interviews, student observations, recent or additional information.)

_____

_____

___Yes   ___No   **15.**   Is the behavior in question caused by, or does it have a **direct** and substantial relationship to the student's disability?

___Yes   ___No   **16.**   Is the behavior the result of something other than the disability? (If yes, indicate the source of the behavior. [e.g., chemical dependency, serious illness, life change event, etc.] [Committee must consider all assessment data available for this question.])

_____

_____

If any of the items 2–11 are answered no, then pertinent information must be considered. It is suggested that manifestation determination would result in behavior being a manifestation of the student's disability due to the LEA's lack of proper creation and/or administration of the IEP. All placement decisions should then be a result of a reconvening of the IEP team to correct deficiencies and adjust placement. (List below items between 1 and 11 which were answered no.)

_____

_____

If item 1 is answered no and/or any of the items 12–14 are answered yes, then previous knowledge about possible behavior problems exist. It is suggested that manifestation determination would yield results indicating that behavior may be a manifestation of the student's disability. This may result from numerous instances, such as recent behavior(s) emerging/evolving patterns not documented or recognized as important previously, or previous treatment/evaluation/assessment results not available when the IEP was written. All placement decisions should then be a result of reconvening the IEP team to correct deficiencies and/or adjust placement. (List below items between 12 and 14 that were answered yes.)

_____

_____

If item 15 is answered yes, then the behavior(s) is/are manifestations of the student's disability. All placement decisions should then be a result of a reconvening of the IEP team to correct deficiencies and/or adjust placement. (Indicate below which item(s) was/were answered yes.)

_____

_____

If all items 1–11 are answered yes, and all items 12–14 are answered no, and item 15 is answered no, then behavior(s) is/are not a manifestation of the student's disability and the student may be disciplined according to the school policy; however FAPE must continue to be provided.

If item 16 is answered yes, then behavior(s) is/are not a manifestation of the student's disability and the student may be disciplined according to the school policy; however, FAPE must continue to be provided.

The IEP team determines that this student's behavior(s) [is/are; is not/are not] a manifestation of his or her disability.   (Circle one)

APPENDIX 8B

BEHAVIOR INCIDENT REPORT AND ANALYSIS

SCHOOL INCIDENT REPORT

Student Name: _____ Person Reporting: _____

Date: _____ Time of Incident: _____ Location of Incident: _____

List all persons present at the time of the incident:

Briefly describe what was happening prior to the incident.

Describe what the student was doing prior to the incident.

Describe in detail what the student did and what happened throughout the incident. Was this incident disruptive, threatening, and/or dangerous?

Briefly describe what happened to the student immediately after the incident. Were there any "consequences" either natural or disciplinary?

School Discipline File Review

Student:_____ DOB: _____

School:_____ Exceptionality: _____

Evaluator:_____ Position: _____ Date: _____

Incidents Recorded	Date	Consequence(s)

Behavior Patterns or Trends Indicated or Noted.

Total number of days suspended to date.

9

What Does a Principal Need to Know About Due Process?

Due process in special education provides parents and school districts an opportunity to ensure children are receiving a free appropriate public education. As a principal, you need to know the parents' rights, the district's rights, the obligations of the parents and of the district, the process, how to prepare for a hearing, what is involved, the principal's role, and what happens when the hearing is over. Your understanding of due process procedures will assist your district in presenting information as accurately as possible, and help to ensure an appropriate education for the student with a disability.

WHAT IS DUE PROCESS?

Parents may request a *due process hearing* to question a school's identification, evaluation, educational placement, or provision of services, relating to their child, or to resolve procedural violations issues. They may also question information on their child's educational records. Recently, there has been an increase in the number of due process hearings regarding disciplinary actions for students with identified disabilities. Due process hearings are not only for parents. Districts may request a due process hearing if parents refuse to consent to the potential evaluation of their child, or they refuse to agree to the placement recommended by the district.

Due process is commonly thought of in terms of a hearing, but it is much more than that. Due process encompasses the legal procedures and requirements enacted by the Individuals with Disabilities Education Act (IDEA; 1990) and state regulations protecting the rights of students with disabilities. It includes the written notices that need to be provided to the parents and the written consent of the parents to evaluation and services provided for their child. All written notices need to be provided to the parents in their native or preferred language, and you must make an effort to schedule

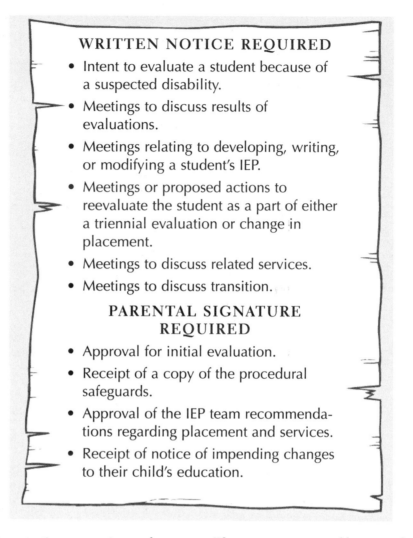

WRITTEN NOTICE REQUIRED

- Intent to evaluate a student because of a suspected disability.
- Meetings to discuss results of evaluations.
- Meetings relating to developing, writing, or modifying a student's IEP.
- Meetings or proposed actions to reevaluate the student as a part of either a triennial evaluation or change in placement.
- Meetings to discuss related services.
- Meetings to discuss transition.

PARENTAL SIGNATURE REQUIRED

- Approval for initial evaluation.
- Receipt of a copy of the procedural safeguards.
- Approval of the IEP team recommendations regarding placement and services.
- Receipt of notice of impending changes to their child's education.

meetings at a time convenient to the parents. (If parents cannot attend because of work or other obligations, you must make an effort to include them, for example via a conference call.)

Providing written notifications as required meets the spirit of the law with the intent of involvement of the parents. It also meets the Supreme Court's definition of appropriateness (in *Henrick Hudson District Board of Education v. Rowley*, 1982).

RECORDKEEPING AND THE PRINCIPAL'S ROLE

The principal is often the one who needs to answer parental questions about education; the education of students with disabilities carries additional recordkeeping requirements and procedures.

✓ Ensure that both the student files and the student's parents have a copy of procedural safeguards. Be able to answer questions about these procedures.

✓ Be available to sit down with parents and discuss contents of student records, individualized education programs (IEPs), related services, and the school's approach to IEP implementation.

✓ Participate in team meetings about student records and test results, and be able to make informed decisions about recommended placement.

✓ Ensure confidentiality of student records.

✓ Document inquiries about the implementation of special education or related services for individual students, and the school's response.

✓ Inform the district special education administrator(s) when there might be a potential problem (perceived or real) in the education of a student with a disability, and know when to ask others for help in solving problems.

IMPARTIAL DUE PROCESS HEARINGS

Due process is a legal term that refers to ensuring that those entitled to goods and services are treated appropriately. Congress included due process as a part of the original Public Law 94-142 (1975) (see Chapter 3) to provide a check on the system providing services to students. *Due process hearings* are the procedure used to resolve differences between parents and the school district. They are formal by nature, with both sides often represented by an attorney, and a stenographer recording every word. They are referred to as *impartial* due process hearings because of the independence the hearing officer brings to the meeting.

The hearing officer cannot be an employee of the district, and may not have any personal or professional matters or interests that call into question her or his objectivity.

Due process hearings take different formats in different states. For example, in Pennsylvania, a state-designated agency appoints a hearing officer, who calls the hearing, runs the hearing, and is the author and disseminator of the decision. By contrast, in Delaware, the hearing is held by a three-person panel: an attorney, a parent, and an educator; the attorney has responsibility for authoring the decision. In California, an administrative law judge (ALJ) hears the case on one day, but may do employment law the next, and workers compensation the third.

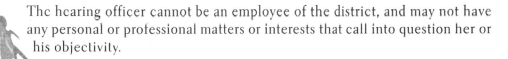

What is the form of your state's due process hearing?

Either the parent or the district can request a due process hearing at any time they feel it is necessary to help resolve a disagreement; no matter who requests the hearing, after the decision has been rendered everyone will have to implement that decision to provide an appropriate education for the student.

The subject of the due process hearing is limited to those issues raised in the due process hearing request (or amended due process hearing request) unless the other party agrees otherwise.

The parent or local education agency (LEA; i.e., the school district) must file a *due process hearing request* within 2 years of the date of the alleged action that forms the basis of the request. There are limited exceptions to this timeline. It does not apply if the parent was prevented from requesting the due process hearing due to specific misrepresentations by the LEA that it had resolved the problem, or if the LEA withheld required information from the parent.

Contents of Due Process Hearing Request

1. The name of the child, the address where the child lives, and the name of the school the child is attending.

2. If the child or youth is homeless, available contact information for the child and the name of the school the child is attending.

3. A description of the nature of the problem, including facts relating to such problem.

4. A proposed resolution of the problem to the extent known and available to the party filing the request.

The due process hearing request is considered to be sufficient unless the party receiving it notifies the hearing officer/ALJ and the other party in writing within 15 days of receipt that the receiving party believes the request does not meet the requirements listed above, and specifies the areas of deficiency. The hearing officer/ALJ must rule on the sufficiency of the request within 5 days of receiving a party's challenge, and must immediately notify both parties in writing of the determination.

The due process hearing request can be amended only if the other party consents in writing to the amendment and is given the opportunity to resolve the issues raised, through a preliminary meeting/resolution session; or the hearing officer grants permission for the party to amend the request, no later than 5 days before a due process hearing occurs.

Responding to a Due Process Hearing Request

If the LEA has not sent a prior written notice to the parent regarding the subject matter contained in the parent's due process hearing request, it must respond within 10 days of receiving the due process hearing request. The response must include an explanation of why the LEA proposed or refused to take the action raised in the request; a description of other options the IEP team considered and the reasons why those options were rejected; a description of the evaluation procedures, assessments, records, or reports used as the basis for the proposed or refused action; and a description of factors relevant to the LEA's proposal or refusal.

Filing this response does not prevent the LEA from challenging the sufficiency of the due process hearing request.

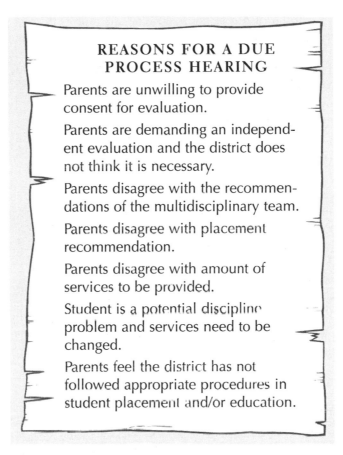

REASONS FOR A DUE PROCESS HEARING

Parents are unwilling to provide consent for evaluation.

Parents are demanding an independent evaluation and the district does not think it is necessary.

Parents disagree with the recommendations of the multidisciplinary team.

Parents disagree with placement recommendation.

Parents disagree with amount of services to be provided.

Student is a potential discipline problem and services need to be changed.

Parents feel the district has not followed appropriate procedures in student placement and/or education.

PRELIMINARY MEETING/RESOLUTION SESSION

Before a due process hearing occurs, and within 15 days of receiving the due process hearing request, the LEA must convene a preliminary meeting with the parent and the relevant member or members of the IEP team with specific knowledge of the facts in the due process hearing request. The goal is to resolve those issues without the need to proceed to a due process hearing. A representative of the LEA who has decision-making authority must be present at this meeting. The LEA may not have an attorney at the meeting unless the parent is also accompanied by an attorney. The parent and the LEA may agree, in writing, to waive this meeting, or agree to use the mediation process.

If the issues in the due process hearing request are resolved at the preliminary meeting, the parent and an authorized LEA representative must sign a written agreement. The agreement is a legally binding document and may be enforced by a court.

Either the parent or LEA may void the agreement within 3 business days of the date of the agreement. After 3 days, the agreement is binding on both parties.

The parent and LEA may agree to use alternative means of meeting participation, such as videoconferences and conference calls.

If the LEA does not resolve the due process hearing request within 30 days of receipt, or within 30 days of receiving an amended due process hearing request, the due process hearing may proceed. The timeline for completion of due process hearings is 45 days, unless the hearing officer/ALJ grants specific extensions of time at the request of either party.

PREPARING FOR A HEARING

All evidence expected to be used in the hearing, and a list of all individuals who might be called to testify, must be made available to both parties at least 5 days before the hearing. You may need to provide copies of all IEPs for the student, all records of meetings with parents, records of evaluation team meetings, psychological reports and assessments, copies of the student's work, and notes from observations.

It is important that you get copies of all requested materials to the attorneys as soon as you learn that a hearing has been requested.

Providing the information as soon as possible will keep the district informed about what has been provided for this student, and may lead to either a quick settlement or easier negotiations if the case goes to mediation.

Parents (and their attorneys) have the right to review all records. It is important to provide the information to the parents, not only because it is their right but because it will provide them a better understanding of their child's educational history. The IDEA regulations state that "the parents of a child with a disability shall be afforded. . . an opportunity to inspect and review all educational records," including those relating to the child's "identification, evaluation, and educational placement," and "the provision of FAPE." [§ 300.501a]

LOGISTICS

Many states hold the due process hearing at the local school or local school administration building. If the due process hearing is being held at your school there are several points that need attention regarding logistical arrangements for the hearing.

- ✓ Is there a meeting room big enough to hold the attendees comfortably? In addition, the temperature of the room should be moderate, seating comfortable, and water and restrooms available.

- ✓ Is the facility accessible for individuals with disabilities?

- ✓ Is the meeting room free of distractions?

- ✓ Is the office support staff aware of the location of the hearing to help direct participants, but also aware of the confidential nature of the process?

- ✓ Is there accessible parking?

- ✓ Have you made plans to cover the classes of attending teachers?

PREPARING TO TESTIFY AT A DUE PROCESS HEARING

To be an effective witness for your school district, you need to fully understand the issue(s) of the hearing. If you are expected to testify, work with the school district's attorney about possible lines of questioning and make sure you can answer potential questions. It is the attorney's responsibility to take a broader, more comprehensive view of the situation. Review the student's file and be prepared to discuss your school's policies. Also, review the documents that will entered by the school district as exhibits.

Your goal is to provide as accurate a picture of the educational programming from the school district's perspective as possible. You should be familiar not only with the educational programming provided to the student in question, but the programs for other students with IEPs at your school.

You should be prepared to answer a variety of questions:

1. What is the student's disability?

2. Is there anybody on the staff who is knowledgeable about the disability?

3. How long has this student attended your school?

4. If this student attended your school in previous years, how successful were other teachers with him or her?

5. Where did they go to school before attending your school?

6. Are there other students with similar disabilities attending your school? Other schools in the district? If so, what types of educational interventions and services do they receive?

7. Is there a clear tie between the assessment report developed for the student and the information contained in their IEP? For example, if the main points of the assessment report identify problems in math, does the IEP have clear goals identifying supports and instruction in math?

8. Is there a clear tie between the information written in the IEP with the actual services provided to the student? (i.e., as written in the IEP, student will receive individual instruction one hour/day, and they are actually only getting 20 minutes. If that is so, then there is a discrepancy and a change either needs to be made to the student's IEP, or a change needs to be made in the amount of instruction provided).

9. Is the student receiving the aides and services included in the IEP? (i.e., student will receive support from an aide three hours/day, but the aide is often helping other teachers or making copies in the school's office).

10. What does the district provide to meet the educational interventions needs of this student?

11. Where does the student receive services? General education class or separate class?

12. How do these educational interventions and services differ from those provided to students who do not have an IEP? Is it just the same information and instruction, but just more of it?

13. What is specially designed about the instruction?

14. Are the educational interventions and services provided to the student by individuals trained in their use? Many schools rely on volunteers or aides, so

it is important to determine if the specially designed instruction provided to this student is by someone trained in its use.

15. Are the educational interventions and services provided by someone certified by the state in the area of disability for which they are working? If not, what certification(s) does this individual hold?

16. How long has the person who is providing the service worked with students with disabilities like this one?

17. Do the educational interventions and services provided have research demonstrating their effectiveness with students who have a similar disability as the one with which the hearing is about? If so, what types of research? Is the research published in reputable journals?

18. Are there other educational interventions or services that could be provided to the student that are more effective? If so, by whom and where?

19. Can you describe the education services this student receives to a lay person? Include the rationale, structure, and specifics of the intervention. For example, can you explain the difference between two different reading programs, clarifying which one is systematic phonics instruction and which one is not?

20. When you observe(d) in the classroom, what is a typical day like for this student? What is a typical day like for the teacher?

21. Is the complaint with the teacher? If so, has this teacher had complaints from students or parents before?

22. If this student is not passing his or her classes, what are the criteria for expectation of passing grades? List these criteria as with and without support.

23. Do the individuals who encounter the student implement modifications written into the IEP? For example, does the student receive untimed tests in all classes delineated in the IEP?

24. Does the student receive the related services they need by someone trained in that specialty?

25. Finally, if the student receives his or her instruction in the general education classroom with supports from a special education teacher, do the general education teacher and the special education teacher meet on a regular basis?

The questions listed above are to assist in preparation of what might be asked. They help to ensure you know all the necessary information before you testify. It is unlikely that you will testify on all the matters addressed in these questions. For example, the teachers who are providing the service to the student would testify on the educational programming. The district's special education supervisor might testify about the provision of services for students with similar disabilities in the district. However, it is important for you to have an understanding of the issues.

TESTIFYING AT THE HEARING

Each individual who testifies is sworn in, and a stenographer records the testimony. The stenographer's job is to record every statement made to help establish a clear and accurate record to assist with the writing of the decision. This record is important for appeals, and helps to assist with implementation after the hearing.

The school district's attorney will have briefed you on the questions they will ask of you, letting you know where your testimony falls as a part of the whole case. After your attorney has asked you the questions as a part of their case, you may be cross-examined by the parents' attorney, or asked questions by the parents themselves. Answer all questions in a straightforward and honest manner; be open to the questions, and answer them truthfully and completely.

One hearing may be all that is necessary. However, if it is a complicated case with multiple or detailed issues, more than one hearing might be needed.

MEDIATION

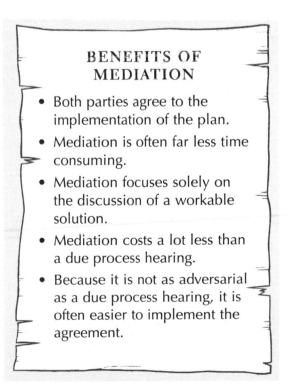

Mediation is a dispute resolution process where the parties work in a collaborative fashion to come to agreement.

Since 1997, voluntary mediation has been a part of IDEA, and this was fully embraced in IDEA 2004. Most states already had a form of mediation as a part of their procedural safeguards. Congress established mediation because many individuals felt due process hearings were too antagonistic, and they wanted another remedy for complaints. Mediation would occur before a due process hearing; it is a valuable part of the process of ensuring the appropriate education of students with disabilities.

There are different methods of using mediation. When there is a dispute over educational programming, many individuals immediately think the only method of solving the problem is to go to a due process hearing. Offer mediation as a means of solving the disputes. Many disputes never make it to an actual hearing because the parties have agreed to the appropriate means of implementation.

In mediation, an impartial individual knowledgeable about the laws assists the two sides in resolving their disputes and to understand each other's viewpoints. It is structured, with each party taking turns in presenting their views, but does not contain the full-blown presentation of facts that are involved in a due process hearing. In mediation, the intent is to focus on resolving conflicts. The third party (mediator) works to help both

BENEFITS OF MEDIATION

- Both parties agree to the implementation of the plan.
- Mediation is often far less time consuming.
- Mediation focuses solely on the discussion of a workable solution.
- Mediation costs a lot less than a due process hearing.
- Because it is not as adversarial as a due process hearing, it is often easier to implement the agreement.

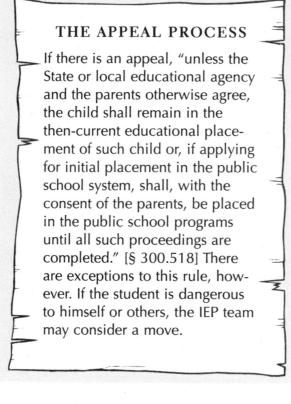

THE APPEAL PROCESS

If there is an appeal, "unless the State or local educational agency and the parents otherwise agree, the child shall remain in the then-current educational placement of such child or, if applying for initial placement in the public school system, shall, with the consent of the parents, be placed in the public school programs until all such proceedings are completed." [§ 300.518] There are exceptions to this rule, however. If the student is dangerous to himself or others, the IEP team may consider a move.

parties agree on a solution that everyone can accept. The difference between mediation and due process is that the mediator has no authority to impose a solution.

The mediator puts the agreement in writing to ensure both parties understand it. Many times as a part of mediation, both parties sign a confidentiality agreement stating they will not talk to others about the problems, the discussion, or the agreement itself.

Your role in mediation depends upon the role you play in the education of the student with a disability. You could be *vital*, participating in the discussion of the problems and the potential solutions. If you are part of the mediation process, unless you are given the authority to sign as the representative of the district, do not sign your name as agreeing to the settlement until you have discussed with your superintendent the agreement and received approval. Your involvement could also be *tangential*. The mediator could be working to come to agreement and when they get close to agreement the representative of the district might come to you and ask if the potential solution is workable. Regardless of the role you play in the mediation process, you have to be available to discuss logistics, and you have to be able to implement the solution in a confidential matter after the agreement.

Although there are clear benefits to mediation, it should not be used to deny parents their access to a due process hearing.

NEVER GETTING TO TRIAL

As noted above, not all due process requests result in a hearing. Just as in many court cases, there are often last-minute agreements. You may very well prepare for many hours, and not be needed on that day. Often on the day of the hearing, the attorneys can narrow the issues down to just one or two that truly need to be addressed.

All is not lost if this happens. By going through this process, you have gained valuable insight into the workings of the special education program in your school, and know more specifically the strengths and weaknesses of the services provided. The knowledge you have gained regarding one student's educational program will assist you in discussions with the parents, the staff, and others in the future.

WHAT HAPPENS WHEN IT IS OVER?

The hearing officer's decision, issued within 15 calendar days after the hearing, is binding on all parties unless it is appealed. (Any appeal must be filed within 15 days of receipt of the decision.) If it is appealed, then the student stays in the current placement until the appeals are completed.

Due process hearings can be antagonistic proceedings. Your professional competence or work ethic might be questioned. The parents may have placed their child in a different school and are requesting reimbursement because they feel your school is terrible and is not meeting their needs. Similarly, negative statements might be made about the parents, such as they just let their child miss too many days of school because they didn't have the energy to bring them, or they repeatedly missed meetings or refused to sign papers or notices.

Regardless of the testimony and documents presented at a due process hearing, after it is over everyone has to work together to meet the needs of the student with a disability. The same parties that may have been sitting on opposite sides of the table arguing through their attorneys over the appropriate education of the student now have to sit together to implement the IEP. The principal's role is to take the lead in ensuring the timely implementation of the decision. If the district has decided not to file an appeal, then the decision of the Hearing Officer needs to be implemented as soon as possible.

Few parents pursue due process because they enjoy the attention or the litigious process. Most due process hearings requested by parents are the result of an honest attempt to provide the best possible education for their child. Your goal throughout this process should be on working with the parents, to ensure the student with a disability receives an appropriate education.

————————————————————————————

Additional Resources

The chapters are intended to summarize and explain the pertinent regulations regarding the education of students with disabilities. For more information, and to read the actual regulations, the following internet sites are provided. Multiple sites are provided in case a site changes or a specific link does not work.

IDEA

Individuals with Disabilities Education Act of 1990, 20 U.S.C. § 1400

Individuals with Disabilities Education Act amendments of 1997

Individuals with Disabilities Education Improvement Act of 2004

IDEA 2004: language: http://frwebgate.access.gpo.gov/cgi-bin/getdoc.cgi?dbname=108_cong_public_laws&docid=f:publ446.108

IDEA: OSEP individual topic links: http://www.ideapartnership.org/whatsnew.cfm

IDEA: Key provisions: http://ojjdp.ncjrs.org/pubs/walls/appen-f.html

IDEA 2004: language: http://frwebgate.access.gpo.gov/cgi-bin/getdoc.cgi?dbname=108_cong_public_laws&docid=f:publ446.108

IDEA: OSEP individual topic links: http://www.ideapartnership.org/whatsnew.cfm

IDEA: Key provisions: http://ojjdp.ncjrs.org/pubs/walls/appen-f.html

http://www.state.nj.us/njded/specialed/idea/reauth/1pagers/

EHA: http://asclepius.com/angel/special.html

NCLB

No Child Left Behind Act of 2001

NCLB: http://www.ed.gov/policy/elsec/guid/edpicks.jhtml?src=fp

Rehab Act (Section 504)

Rehabilitation Act of 1973, Pub. L. No. 93-112, 29 U.S.C. § 701 et seq

Section 504 regulations (34 C.F.R. § 104.35(b))

Rehab Act: http://www.section508.gov/index.cfm?FuseAction=Content&ID=15

Americans with Disabilities Act (ADA)

Americans with Disabilities Act of 1990, Pub. L. No. 101-336, 42 U.S.C. § 12101 et seq

http://www.sba.gov/ada/adaact.txt

http://www.eeoc.gov/facts/fs-ada.html

http://www.dol.gov/esa/regs/statutes/ofccp/ada.htm

Family Educational Rights and Privacy Act (FERPA)

Family Educational Rights and Privacy Act of 1974, 20 U.S.C. § 1232g

FERPA: http://www.ed.gov/policy/gen/guid/fpco/ferpa/index.html or http://www.epic.org/privacy/education/ferpa.html

Elementary and Secondary Education Act of 1965

Elementary and Secondary Education Act of 1965

Improving America's Schools Act of 1994

NCLB Guidelines, Federal Register, March 20, 2005

ESEA: http://www.ed.gov/policy/elsec/leg/esea02/beginning.html#sec6

Improving Schools Act: http://www.ed.gov/legislation/ESEA/toc.html

Code of Federal Regulations: http://www.gpoaccess.gov/cfr/index.html

For additional updates on public policy visit the Council for Exceptional Children website at www.cec.sped.org/pp/

Bibliography

Americans With Disabilities Act of 1990, Pub. L. No. 101-336, 42 U.S.C. § 12101 *et seq.* (West).

Beck, A. T., Steer, R. A., Brown, G. K. (1996). *Beck Depression Inventory.* Orlando, FL:

Bettlcheim, B. (1967). *The empty fortress.* New York: Free Press.

Brown, L. & Hammill, D. D. (1990). *Behavior Rating Profile (BRP-2).* Austin: Pro-Ed.

Cedar Rapids Community School District v. Garrett F., 119 S. Ct. 992 (1999)

Conners, C. K. (1997). *Conners' Rating Scale-Revised,* North Tonawanda, NY: MHS.

Education of All Handicapped Children Act of 1975, Pub. L. No. 94-142.

Elementary and Secondary Education Act of 1965, Pub. L. No. 84

Greer v. Rome City School District, 950 F. 2d 688

Gresham, F. M. & Elliott, S. N. (2000). *SSRS: Social Skills Rating System.* Circle Pines, MN: AGS.

Henrick Hudson District Board of Education v. Rowley 458 U.S. 176, 181, 1982.

IDEA Federal Regulations 34 C.F.R. § 300.532.

Individuals with Disabilities Education Act Amendments of 1997 (IDEA). Pub. L. No. 105-17, 20 U. S. C. § 1400 et seq. (1997).

Individuals With Disabilities Education Act of 1990, 20 U.S.C. § 1400 *et seq.* (West).

McCarney, S. B., & Arthaud, T. J. (2003). *The Emotional or Behavior Disorders Scale (EBDS-R)* (Rev. ed.). Columbia, MO: Hawthorne Educational Services.

McCarney, S. B., & Arthaud, T. J. (2005). *Behavior Evaluation Scale (BES-3:L)* (3rd ed.). Columbia, MO: Hawthorne Educational Services.

McCarney, S. B. (2004). *The Attention Deficit Disorders Evaluation Scale (ADDES-3)* (3rd ed.). Columbia, MO: Hawthorne Educational Services.

National Association of School Psychologists. (2003). Psychological evaluations: What every principal should know. *Principal Leadership Magazine*, 4(3).

National Association of School Psychologists. (2003). Position Statement on School Psychologists' Involvement in the Role of Assessment. Available: www.nasponline.org/information/pospaper_assess.html

National Commission on Excellence in Education. (1983) *A nation at risk: The imperative for educational reform.* Washington, DC: U.S. Department of Education.

No Child Left Behind Act of 2001 (NCLB), Pub. L. No. 107-110

Oberti v. Board of Education (995 F.2d 1204 (3rd Cir. 1993) 19 IDELR 908).

Rehabilitation Act of 1973, Pub. L. No. 93-112, 29 U.S.C. § 701 et seq. (1973).

Reynolds, C. R. & Kamphaus, R. W., BASC-2 Behavior Assessment for Children. (2004). Circle Pines, MN: AGS.

Roncker v. Walker, 700 F. 2d 1058 (6th Cir., 1983)

Sacramento Unified School District v Rachel H., 14 F.3d 1398 (9th Cir. 1994)

Section 504 of the Rehabilitation Act of 1973, 29 U.S.C. § 794 et seq. (West).

Section 504 Regulations (34 C.F.R. § 104.35(b))

Shapiro, E. S. (2004a). *Academic skills problems: Direct assessment and intervention* (3rd ed.), NY: Guilford.

Shapiro, E. S. (2004b). *Academic skills problems workbook* (Rev. ed.), NY: Guilford.

West, R. R. (2002). The fallacy behind increased accountability: How disabled students' constitutional rights have been disregarded in a rush to implementing high-stakes exams. Brigham Young University Education and Law Journal, 2, 351-362.

www.nasponline.org/information/pospaper_assess.html

Yell, M. L. & Drasgow, E. (2005). *No Child Left Behind: A guide for professionals.* Upper Saddle River, NJ: Pearson Merrill Prentice Hall.

Index